THE
Divine
Source Within

Conscious Creation, Law of Attraction
and Manifestation

SPIRIT WALKER

ISBN: 1468120867
ISBN 13: 9781468120868

Contents

Introduction

Namaste. The first thing the conscious mind will want to do is judge. The judge in you will want to judge the contents of this book. If you spend your time judging this book, you will not learn a thing. You will not be present.

We are all beautiful souls. I have been working as a Spiritual Life Coach and a Clinical Hypnotherapist for many years. The content in this book is true and has been used by myself and many others to create a blissful life. As you read the book, you will find centers of your BEING open naturally and LIGHT begin to transform into your life.

The information in this book contains high Divine Source energy. Just by reading this book, things will unfold and begin to manifest for you without even trying. The High Council has asked me to distribute this material. I am only a "hallow bone" as the Shamans say, or a vessel for the purpose of Divine wisdom to flow. This means that the energy contained within this book will activate, accelerate and/or align you to the connection of your soul and The Source's wisdom. This knowledge also lies within our DNA. As a disclaimer, these frequencies have the potential to greatly accelerate your awakening process and the activation of your divine blueprint...your birthright.

What you can use this book for...

"We are not human beings on a spiritual journey. We are spiritual beings on a human journey."

STEPHEN R. COVEY

This Divine book can be used for attracting:

- Love
- Good Health
- Business and Money
- A peaceful and blissful life
- Changing your behavioral patterns associated with your DNA
- Creating a better world to live in
- Living your birthright, your soul's blueprint.

Most of all, it is about you. It is about the love and light in you that can change your outer world.

Important note: The author is not responsible for any use or action taken by whomever reads this book. Information in this book is wisdom and any who use it for the purpose toward manifesting a better life is completely and solely the reader's responsibility.

Namaste,

Spirit Walker

CHAPTER ONE

What you will learn

"The Basis of Your Life is Freedom; the Purpose of Your Life is Joy"

ABRAHAM-HICKS

The power to consciously imagine, create and attract that which you intend.

It is your subconscious mind that is the storehouse of your deep-seated beliefs and programs. To change your circumstances and attract to yourself that which you choose, you must come to understand your DNA process and your thoughts.

You will learn to program and re-program awareness, dis-creating and re-creating through gratitude, meditation, present moment and creative visualization. **It is the technique underlying reality creation, making use of thought power to consciously imagine, create and attract that which you intend.** Your imagination is the part of the Divine software you were birthed with and is your birthright. It converts your thought power into mental images, which are in turn manifested in the physical realm.

To stand, sit, and walk in your own creative power with the ability to create and manifest is a blessing. The Divine Creator created us in his image and that is to create beautiful things, express beautiful, sacred love and heal each other.

This book contains messages so that you can work from the very beginning on your current thought process, clearing unwanted negative programming (clearing the slate) and reprogramming through thought, visualization, imagination (your dream world) and the Law of Attraction. Through this program you will understand Gratitude and *the magic* it delivers, the power of thought, the power of your subconscious mind, the conscious mind, discreate and re-create, and the Law of Attraction/Manifestation.

CHAPTER TWO

The Divine in YOU

*"Your talent is God's gift to you. What you do
with it is your gift back to God"*

-LEO BUSCAGLIA

"Praise the bridge that carried you over."

-GEORGE COLEMAN

You have to realize what you are: a divine light BEING. It is what we all are, always have been and always will be. The only problem is that we have forgotten it, and now we identify with all kinds of concepts about ourselves that we have created with our mind. We think we are this and we think we are that, but these are all artificial beliefs we have built along the way. They are not what we are. Yes, we 'have' a personality, given to us at birth. But this personality is like a cover we have put on, it is like a vehicle we got to drive around in this physical world. As we forgot we are the driver, we have identified with the vehicle. You have to remember again that you are the driver. The personality, the cover or vehicle, is a means of expressing ourselves here on earth, but we should not identify with it. We have to feel and become aware of our true selves: the divine light beings we are.

As we are part of the Divine, we can bring this Divine essence into our everyday awareness. This Divine essence has Divine blessings and power. Therefore, every day you should not only pay attention to your thinking, but you should also make yourself aware that you are a divine light-BEING. This can easily be done by visualization. Imagine or see yourself in your human form but composed solely of divine light. Change your way of thinking, expressions, and how you consciously manifest. Work as a WHOLE, not just what benefits you. Create also what will benefit others. You are a spiritual BEING in your physical body and your essence is part of the WHOLE. Your inner Being is a part of this entire Universe. It's that simple and quite effective. You may not be able to keep that image in your mind every second, but you can by living and being present as much as you possibly can.

When your active imagination or meditation is over, place the light images in the back of your mind and during the day try to remember as often as you can that you are this light BEING. I know, by experience, that after a while we get lazy and start to forget about it. We are all lazy beings at times, but in actuality, it's more about habits. We are all habitual and conditioned by our environment to only pay attention to mundane things. You cannot give up; you have to make an effort to become that light BEING you really are. Life will only get better for you.

"I am" has a lot of power. BEING in the "I am" state of heart and mind, you are in the present moment. Every blessing, every dream that you desire should be created in the present moment. Being present is the best place you can be to consciously create. "I am" has Divine Power BEING! The "I am" is who you really are. The more you understand being present in your "I am" seat, the more you gain power in your present BEING.

Becoming your birthright is essentially divine. This is the SEAT where you should always operate from. If you want to be creative and successful, then you must get the power! The power is within all of us. There are conceptual beliefs that by getting power means we might become equal or greater than the Divine. No, I am not speaking about greed power here. Greed power is selfish. Divine power is selfless.

Divine power is higher consciousness and the super-subconscious, working together, side by side. It's awakening to your higher purpose to serve the Divine and the Light. **A**wakened, **L**ove, **E**nlightenment, **E**mpowerment, **P**urity, and **T**ruth are all for the purpose of your higher BEING. Higher purpose is your Divine call, your birthright seat. No one can claim it but you.

I have come across many humans who say they are powerless and they are only the vehicle in which the Divine chooses to work through. Great! But if you are not driving that vehicle and standing in your Divine power, then you are not flowing in Divine consciousness. You are then only a seed that has not fully blossomed or awakened.

When we accept to live by conditions rather than Divine flow, we will not connect to the higher wisdom. To be a vehicle or hallow bone for the Divine, one must understand gratitude and the leverage of the conscious mind. Gratitude carries weight in the universe. It magically opens doors and mirrors back to you more opportunities on all you are grateful for and more. I will discuss more of this in *Chapter Four, The Magic of Gratitude*.

We would all love to be beyond the conscious mind, but there is not one human on earth that has not carried some conditional belief in their DNA. When we dis-create the negative of our DNA, we begin to feel a much higher knowledge and wisdom. When we let go of our belief system and adhere to the silence of our breath, we are in the Divine seat. We are present. We are not veiled by negative thoughts or deeds. We live in truth.

Your visions that are created from your Divine birthright or blueprint will be honored and blessed. Your blueprint is your birth map. From this strong and pure base, you will be able to create heaven on earth. There is the Law of Vibration, what is above is below and what is below is above. From there we create the Cause and Effect. What you create mentally (Cause), becomes your outer world (Effect). Your outer world is what you are within. Change within you, your outer world changes. We allow our Ego to dis-create the beauty of our birth. The Divine light BEINGS we are meant to be. We do not dis-create the ill behavior of our Egos but we dis-create the beauty of our essence.

If you take a good look around you, we are self-destructing. We are responsible for our actions that originate from our thoughts. Our planet suffers for this reason. We must join as one conscious thought, and that is Love, Peace, and Light. One soul cannot carry the essence alone. We are responsible together, in unity for our creative thoughts and actions. This is where we are all part of the WHOLE.

There are millions of us on this planet. I want to say ninety percent of you, give up. That's a very high percentage! You see war and hatred and some of you say, "What can I do? Or...what can we do about it?" What can you do about it? It begins with you! Your vibration alone makes a difference as thought does transfer. Life Coach and Creator of the Holistic Learning Center, Hu Dalconzo, created the phrase, "One soul at a time, beginning with mine." If it doesn't live in you, how will you teach another to awaken? Never mind the one who doesn't want to listen and understand their conscious foibles. You take the action and change your thought behavior. You can't change people. They must do the work to change. But what you can give them is a piece of the Light to take with them so that they can touch their inner blueprint, their Divine seat. It's their choice.

You can choose to live in darkness or you can choose to live in Light. How you direct your vehicle as the driver will depend on the creation of your world. As a light worker and teacher, I have seen many souls return to the light within and overcome darkness. Polarity is within every living being. Our makeup is both light and dark. If we want a brighter world, we must choose to be Light.

Trust your intuition. That inner knowing can speak a lot of truth. You are traveling with the Universe, you are never alone. The Universe lives within you. We have returned to rebirth on this planet and heal our karma. We live as a whole. Other people's deeds can affect both us and our planet. How we consciously create is very important. How we become conscious of our thoughts, actions and even becoming aware of what is unconscious has a very important effect on the world. We are here to self master our way back home to the Divine and the Universe. We all depart some time or another. What we learn, share, teach and absorb returns with us when we depart.

We are taught to suffer. In the human Book of Knowledge, we have been taught by our caretakers that to suffer is God's intention. We cannot feel the purity of God if we are suffering. Darkness in this world has taught us that we must suffer for the Divine in order to find the Light. No more suffering! Suffering is Ego! The first to admit that suffering must be obtained in order to be spiritual is in Ego. The ones who still generate their energy, thoughts, love and power through Ego are the ones who suffer. Awakening to your suffering will bring you to self master and home to your birthright.

We are thankful to have so many beautiful, spiritual teachers writing books, giving lectures and workshops to help us all live in the present moment. Let go of the past and be conscious of your thoughts and actions. Live within gratitude and abundance and so will become your outer world.

I am certainly proud to live my Divine birthright. I am forever grateful in gratitude and abundance for our Creator. But I am not perfect. I, too, can jump out of the Driver's seat and become the vehicle. Through meditation and silence, sitting in present moment, I have learned to comprehend the triggers leading me deeper into the dark adversary that lives also within me. As there is light within, there is also dark within. You choose which way you want to live. If you want happiness, the light is the only way. By being conscious of these triggers, you will recognize these negative traits and find your way back to the essential Light. Everything we do, from work to play, we are ONE with our breath, our Light, our Aum (Ohm) within. When you are ONE with your BEING (Be-in-GOD-Self) with impeccability in what and how you think, speak, feel, and act...you will have the Divine Light within.

So how does one become the "I am"? How does one become whole? Remember, it's not how you become, as you are naturally this. It is awakening that will begin to center you in the "I am". However, the first adversary that needs to go is your EGO! I call it the "adversary" as it represents a person, group, or force that opposes or attacks. Ego opposes within us and creates and Ego world. You cannot be "I am" in Ego. "I am" is present. Ego is not. Ego will have you here and there and everywhere beside present. It has only known what it has experienced and will have you suffer within the memory of pain, and sorrow. The Ego will have you acting a dual role, the Judge and the Victim.

Your words must be impeccable. When someone speaks to you, you need to listen with a sharp ear. You do not have to accept what someone says to you, but most people will accept the first words someone will speak. We are a communicable planet. Once you accept it, you become it. You begin to believe it. Your mind (head) will transfer it down to the mind in your solar plexus. Behind the stomach and liver is your physical mind. You become the believer of that knowledge and it affects you both mentally and physically. Your emotional body reacts.

What is knowledge? It is words and definitions passed on by our caretakers. It is the *Book of Human Law.* My suggestion is to throw that book away. It consists of judgment, conditional love, control and all Human Ego. The true book is the *Book of Essence.* This is the light of your BEING. What you think, you will create. This is manifestation.

A good example is about a girl who plays the flute. She begins to play with beauty and surety. Her mother or father or even a friend says to the girl that she is not good at playing the flute. The mental judge is at play here. Maybe she missed a chord or played off tune. Being innocent and believing her caretakers or friends, she puts down the flute and believes that she cannot play at all. She goes years without being in her Divine birthright because she accepted the power of the word that she cannot play the flute. In her mind, her own judge agrees with the ones who have passed judgment upon her and she becomes the victim. What she may have been born to express in this world, she no longer believes is true. So she goes on in life not believing or acting upon her blueprint. It is so important that you believe in yourself. Believe in your abilities as this is your light and your beliefs help you create. You will receive resistance from the Universe if that belief does not resonate light in return. You will see, feel and receive the messages.

You do not have to accept all things. When someone throws you darkness, words that are not impeccable, words that cause pain, suffering, guilt and so on- why would you want to accept this? Why? We are conditioned to expect and receive the worst. We accept suffering inevitable. I am only here to serve my karma, love is not for me, everyone uses me, and it keeps going on. That is the Ego. You chose this birth, and all the conditions and unconditional designs of it. Through our DNA, we have been integrated in the Book of Human Laws. It is within, that must change and from that change, empower our inner essence to master the Laws rather than the bliss. We are conditioned to accept negativity. We are conditioned to play the role of the Judge and the Victim. We are conditioned to play the role of Caretaker and Savior. It's in our DNA. We operate from the Book of Laws. The Book of Laws is our Human handbook and we all operate from it most of the time. Even *Eckhart Tolle* in "*The Power of Now*" mentions that we allow our Egos to master us and control our lives. Our Ego is an amazing powerful and mental tool. If you allow your Spirit to master your Ego, you will feel a blissful life. Your Ego does not die, but merges in balance with Spirit in Self Mastery.

Life is hard, the world is crazy, the end of the world is of the Universe. Our souls know this by birth. It's only a matter of dis-creating out of the Book of Human Laws and return to the Laws of the Universe. We are born with lessons already designed to manifest and we also create new ones along the way. The lessons are expressed between the Spirit and the Ego. It's hard to accept and learn lessons when Ego is in the driver's seat. Return and become that beautiful Spirit within you. This is the driver's seat. Empower your vehicle.

"I am" is your Spirit. Ego is your mind's adversary, the heavy thinker, the procrastinator, the defender, the opinionated, the dark one and so on. Spirit is the essence of you. Spirit is a natural flow and connected to your birthright. It is the real you. There is nothing you have to go and search for when you are in Spirit. Spirit rightfully merges with your God-Self and will steer you away from BEING your Divine blueprint. BEING is not mind alone. It is beyond mind. It is your higher self, higher super consciousness and super subconscious. They work together. If you can go beyond the Ego (conscious) of the mind, and you can, you will become your natural BEING. BE-IN=GOD/DIVINE. This is your birthright, your blueprint and your bliss.

In Hindu, they say Namaste. 'Namaste' or 'namaskar' is the Indian way of greeting each other. Wherever they are – on the street, in the house, in public transport, on vacation or on the phone, they greet in, "Namaste". Whether it is someone they know or a stranger whom they want to initiate a conversation, Namaste is the customary courtesy greeting to begin with and often to end with. It is not a superficial gesture or a mere word, and is for all people - young and old, friends and strangers. It is my favorite as the Aum–Light (Divine) is present in all of us.

Here is the meaning of *Namaste*:

The God/Goddess within me acknowledges the God/Goddess within you. The Divine in me recognizes and honors, the Divine in you. The spirit within me bows to the spirit within you. I greet that place where you and I are one. I honor the place in you which is of love, of truth, of light and of peace.

How much more beautiful can that be? If all of us believed and honored this light in every one of us and everywhere we go, even blessing the

Universe with light and honor, look at how much Light would shine within us? Imagine what divinity it would create in our world.

Here is the simplicity on how to greet with, "*Namaste*". Bend the arms from the elbow upwards and face the two palms of the hands. Place the two palms together and keep the folded palms in front of the chest (heart). Utter the word, "*Namaste,*" and while saying the word bow the head slightly and close your eyes briefly as this connects you to the Spirit of each other through the Divine. I will do this to greet the Sun, the energy around me before and after meditation or prayer. I do this with everyone I greet, even if I do not use the hand form. Silently, I greet with *Namaste*.

Namaste could be just a casual or formal greeting, a cultural convention or an act of worship. However, there is much more to it than meets the eye. The real meeting between people is the meeting of their mind and heart. When we greet one another with *Namaste*, it means, 'may our mind and heart meet', indicated by the folded palms placed before the chest (heart). The bowing down of the head is a gracious form of extending friendship in love, respect and humility.

The reason why we do *Namaste* has a deeper spiritual significance. It recognizes the belief that the life force, the divinity, the Self or the God in me is the same in all. Acknowledging this oneness with the meeting of the palms, we honor the God in the person we meet. It is the recognition of the divinity within us and extending a warm welcome to each other.

CHAPTER THREE

The Mastery of Divine Love

*"A heart filled with love is like a phoenix that
no cage can imprison."*

~ RUMI

How powerful is this Divine LOVE? Only true love can bring happiness. No other love exists in the Divine heart. When you love unconditionally, you obtain great Divine Power within. Sharing this love with humanity in your thoughts and manifestation is true *BLISS*. Yes, love is the father of Divine magic.

Love must be treated like Divine. Bargaining for love, selling your soul for love, forcing another to love should never exist. When we let our hearts love in purity, our thoughts and creation become pure bliss and truth. See how this beautiful love makes for a Divine life, one filled with laughter, hope, faith and dreams? When you send out love, love returns to you. We can love anyone we care to love as long as the love flows freely and unconditionally. Once you put conditions on this love, it is no longer happy. It's not the same love we were born with. It therefore, can become confined and miserable.

Many do not understand the freedom of love. They think by conditioning love, they can keep it for good. Why would you want to keep it in prison, confine and lust after it, claim it as if it were some materialistic good that can only be bought with money and greed? When love flows freely, that is when it lives forever in you. It always flows within and then out, to return within. Would you not want love as such? Would you not want love to always be within you where you don't have to search for it? When you send out love, it's not important who sends it back to you. What's important is that Divine love flows to all who flourish and honor it. The Universe mirrors back to you this beautiful love. What you give, you get back. This is truth.

You have to understand this love. This beautiful, divine light has no boundaries. Its ravishing breath never dies. Pure love can't exist in a world of selfishness, greed and imprisonment. It must travel freely, from boundless elements to worlds beyond ours.

Give the sacred love of divinity a chance to flourish. Let it live within you. You know this love only too well. It's your birthright, embraced in your blueprint of who you are. Allow it to give you a life of bliss and happiness. Let it put a smile on your heart so that when you shine your light in every space of life, it glows from your face and lightens up another. You will feel a difference it makes in your life. Do not worry if another can't accept this purity. It's not your responsibility to force another to love freely. You just go on being this love and let it go where it will go, flow where it will flow, be what it is to be and shower and heal all that accept it. If it tries to control and imprison you, you will know then it is not true love.

As a conscious creator, it's the emotion of love and respect that empowers deep within us and this empowerment creates pure thought. If you love from the beginning of creation, there is no limit in what you can do for yourself and others. When we love conditionally, with boundaries of greed and selfishness, our creations are not pure nor do they have any substantial light to bless our life-force within. We tread along a path of slow agony, like a lonely death, slowly lose energy and our world becomes bleak and grim. We lose love and happiness. We lose empowerment and gain Ego. We gain a lonely heart. When we love with a pure heart, we gain love in return. True love never dies. It goes with you wherever you go and even when your life ends in this world.

I know you may have been hurt. Hurt so bad that you feel your love transformed to hate. You claim that love is not for you and so therefore you set your thoughts to match the thorns that pricked your heart. And then what happens? You can't feel love, even if it were right in front of your heart. All you can feel is bitterness and you've gone now to label it against humanity, and anyone who offers their heart to you. What a shame. Can't you see why you cry at night, pound the pavement, searching consistently for happiness that never comes to you because you closed off your heart? You closed off the Divine love you were born with. You guarded and protected a love that doesn't exist and pushed away true love that no man or woman can possibly give you without showering that pure love on yourself first.

How can you offer love to another, when you can't even love yourself? I am not talking about loving yourself as if to bargain with it. That is not love. I am talking love yourself freely, no conditions, let love flow and let it return to you like a warm embrace that has no arms, no walls, no layers of control. It has no limitations or boundaries. It doesn't stop flowing because you let it flow like a river that empties in an open body of water such as an ocean or lake and it never has an ending. This is the so-called sea of love. It has no ending because it lives in you, returns to you and is a part of your breath. Your breath keeps sending out more love.

Can you feel the endless power of love in what I am saying to all of you? You are the bounty, the openness, the channel of love that never stops. When we become this pure love, this unconditional essence, then there is no pain. Even when we may be disappointed that love may have failed us in another, there is no such thing. Love never fails you, only the one who does not purely love. How can love fail in true Spirit? Only love fails in mind of Ego.

Love all living things. Love yourself, love nature, love people, love animals, love all space, love all elements, love Mother Earth, love the Universe, and love your Divine Father and Mother. Love, love and LOVE! It begins always with you, never with another. All begins within you. Love cannot be found in your outer world until love has been found within you. Live in this pure love…this true love. Live, give and give more. What you give, you shall receive. Why would you not want to give this unconditional and blessed love to another when you know deep within you, there is no other life? This is what so many are in search of. The reason they have not found it is because they are searching the world to find it and it's been within them all along. Love is LIFE and Life is LOVE. Bless and honor this gift.

CHAPTER FOUR

The Magic of Gratitude

A quote from Mad Bear, a native Indian medicine man, I found in the book Rolling Thunder by Doug Boyd: *"The purpose of good medicine is to make it simple. There is no need to create any opposing destructive force; that only makes more negative energy and more results and more problems. If you have a sense of opposition - that is, if you feel contempt for others - you are in a perfect position to receive their contempt. The idea is not to be a receiver...."*

So what is missing in your life that does not make the *Law of Attraction* work with what you really desire for your dream world? Gratitude is being grateful for what you already have, knowing better times and things are on the way! Beautiful soul magic lies within this Divine secret!

"Feeling grateful or appreciative of someone or something in your life actually attracts more of the things that you appreciate and value into your life."

NORTHRUP CHRISTINE

Yes, we all touch on the stage of saying thank you to everyone for all the beautiful things they have done for us. How about thanking you for being a part of this creation? More importantly, how about thanking everything we have in our lives today, this very moment. I bet you never thought that complaining about things going wrong creates a negative vibration. The Law of Vibration always resonates back to you. So the more you complain, the more you have created a manifestation of exactly what you were complaining about.

So how do we turn things around? We start by complaining less, appreciating what we have by accepting things for how they are in this moment. Apply the finishing touch by knowing that good times are on their way.

The first thing we avoid is change. We get comfortable complaining and begin to accept suffering rather than accepting what we have. How many times have we said, "I don't have enough"? How many times have we said, "Why is life so hard"? The secret is this! Without gratitude, you may be successful, but at one time or another, you will change the success to suffering. Yes, suffering because you did not acknowledge gratitude for your success. The Universe wants acknowledgement for what it has resonated back to you. Your soul is a fragment of the Universe. Gratitude is the missing link that keeps the Law of Vibration consistently working on your behalf.

Gratitude brings us happiness. It is the Divine Light within us. If gratitude can bring you happiness and good then you will attract more good. We create our experiences. I know that as your birthright you wish to create more happiness, love, abundance and achieve even financial security. If we are grateful for what we have, this creates abundance.

"As each day comes to us refreshed and anew, so does my gratitude renews itself daily. The breaking of the sun over the horizon is my grateful heart dawning upon a blessed world."

TERRI GUILLEMETS

In the process of being in gratitude, know what you want and know what you do not want. Be grateful for all you have. Be grateful with much gratitude for all you have currently. The past is gone. It no longer exists so do not reach out to connect with it. Feel all that you have presently. Feel the beauty in everything, even any losses you may have experienced. There may be lack of understanding for your losses but understand they happened for your higher purpose. We also experience and do not understand what we create unconsciously. There are hidden feelings and thoughts that we may not be aware of. For example, how we can lose business.

We can lose business because it does not resonate in our Law of Vibration, either because we unconsciously canceled it or it was not for our higher *BEING*. How do we unconsciously cancel business? There are many reasons. It could be that we do not love what we do. Without *LOVE*, all fades. We do not believe in ourselves or the business we are proposing. The list can go on. Remember, your thoughts begin your creation. This goes for everything we are, do and become. Our outer world is a reflection of our inner world and vice versa. If an unconscious thought does create, be aware always within and your outer world. You will certainly catch any unconscious action through awareness.

Even if your abode is empty, be grateful as material possession is not your Divine Being/Light. Look around you. I know it may be difficult to understand this when your house may have foreclosed, loss in stocks and bonds, a loved one passed away, you lost your job and the list of losses can go on. We cannot prevent Mother Nature, but we can create the energy of gratitude and know that we are blessed. Even though these losses may be happening in your world, do not let them become you. When we absorb loss, we blame ourselves or another.

Repetitive loss is linked to our thinking and somewhere in our thought process we have attracted more loss. There are many who have not lost but have gained. It is a matter of where you are in the complaint world, where you are in your negative thinking world. Even with loss, be in gratitude. Sometimes we go through a cleansing in life and it hits us hard when we are not grateful for what we already have. When you experience loss, you can be grateful for this. I know this might sound silly-why would anyone want to be grateful for losing the shirt off their back? But when we are grateful for a loss, the energy of loss will change to gain. You will gain love, peace and attract beautiful things to you. As much as it might seem different to let go of pain because of your losses, the more you hold on to the pain, the less grateful you are and the more you attract in pain. When we return to painful memories, the memories are like they happened yesterday. They get stronger and more alive because you are feeding energy to that thought process. By not being grateful, the more pain you will feel. Remember that your thoughts create your experience.

By being in gratitude, know that all good things will come. See and feel in gratitude all that you have accomplished. Understand that gratitude is something you already possess. Yes I know, it often doesn't feel that way, especially as the worldview is set up to encourage all of us to fear that there is not enough to be grateful for. You will start to feel more relaxed, have less stress; you will feel more love in your relationships. A good side effect to this magic is you will feel more confident.

We all live heretic lives these days. Having negative thoughts and feelings interrupt the flow of energy that is used in the manifestation of your desires. If you want to be successful in business, have love, and all the good in life, you must apply the law of gratitude. This one law often gets over looked and misunderstood. You can't rhyme with the Law of Attraction without the magic of gratitude. The magic is all around you, the trick is living it.

Know what you do want.

Abundance

To know what you want is very important in conscious creation and manifestation (Law of Attraction). Appreciating what you already have and being grateful in abundance can assist you in attracting more abundance in your life. I am not saying you should become materialistic to understand the power behind how you achieved what you have. Sometimes we feel we need more when we do not. By becoming aware in gratitude of what you already have presently teaches you to really focus on what you truly want from within.

When you focus on what is good and working for you, you are apt to create more. Your thoughts are positive and the law of attraction is at work. If you send something out in thought and you become aware that is not what you want, say to yourself, "cancel", "cancel that", or, "clear". The faster you cancel a negative thought, the less chance to manifest. Focusing on the good things in gratitude will continue to open new avenues and doors for you.

Our thoughts create our world.

You better believe it! The energy + emotion + power applied to the Law of Vibration behind a thought can be very powerful. This vibration flows down from the Mental-Spiritual plane to the astral plane. In the astral plane it begins to take sub-physical shape. It forms and gathers atoms and molecules and then proceeds down to matter (physical) through gravity and manifests. If, by chance, you find that it has not manifested, then there is something within your thought process that is holding it back, preventing the thought and visual process from manifesting. Sometimes what we want to manifest is not in harmony with our soul.

Be pure in your thoughts through gratitude. This way you are conscious in purity of all you create. Have you ever heard the truth about releasing thought and others react? When you send out your thoughts, they become transparent and float through the Universe. If you do not claim what you have consciously created, then when you manifest it and don't take action, another will. I once told a girlfriend about a book I wanted to write many years ago. I told her the creation of the story to the very end. A year later, a movie was made identical to my thought and creation of the story. Remember thoughts created are energy and manifest. I had never acted upon writing it.

Take responsibility for your actions

If you don't act, then it goes to someone willing to act. When we manifest, we must be prepared to take action. Nothing is handed to us on a silver platter. This is called the Law of Vibration and resonates with the Law of Cause and Effect. Know that when you send a thought out, be responsible for this thought. An example would be when sending love, know that the love will spread across the globe and bring blessings and enlightenment to all who receive it. Feel blessed to have created this thought. If you have fallen in love with someone, if you do not take action and express it, it will not manifest fully and you will be disappointed. When sending a negative thought such as hate, expect hate in return. Our world is a perfect example of both love and hate. The destruction of our planet is the prime thought that hate exists beyond love. Let us create loving thoughts and send it to our planet, humanity and to our Universe. Let us all become *ONE* in the conscious process of healing our planet. Just like anything else we create, if we do not bless and love it, it will fade away. It withers and dies. The rebirth is present in everything living. So is death. There are always beginnings and endings. Our life and all living life are precious. Our planet is self destructing because we do not give her enough love, care and respect. She, too, needs to be nurtured, just like us. Our feet are planted on this earth. She feels every vibration of ours. She absorbs our thoughts and actions. Let our thoughts be the creation of gratitude. Gratitude is Divine Blessings.

According to the Indian philosophy "Advaita- Vedanta", which is called "Nonduality" in the West, the world is not real, but only an illusion created by our thoughts. Since most people think and repeat the same or similar thoughts often, focusing their mind and thoughts on their current environment, they create and recreate the same sort of events or circumstances. This process preserves the same "world" and status quo. It is like watching the same film over and over again, but we can change the film by changing our thoughts and visualize different circumstances and life, and in this way create a different "reality". For us, it is a reality, though in fact it is just a dream we call "reality".

What you are within creates your outer world.

When you are grateful within, it shows in the outer world. You attract into your life what you are within. For example, people who have experienced trauma attract in others with similar history. Also, if trauma is not discreated, then you will attract more traumas. Same goes for love. If you are this beautiful unconditional love within, you will attract the same. Everything thought within is a creation in your outer world. Like attracts more like. When you change and become grateful for all you are within and have, do not be surprised if the negative energy that once lived in your dream world falls to the wayside. They may just disappear and leave your circle of friends.

Although this may be a sad time for you, this is also a time of great manifestation. Be grateful for the blessings of Divine Gratitude.

What are you creating today?

Exactly! What are you creating in the present moment? Or are you creating in the present moment? Think about this. Are you living in a past memory of pain, and judgment? Or are you creating beauty in present moment? Are you creating love or hate and what level is your mind when creating this emotional energy? Are you creating good health or illness? Are you creating success or failure? Ask yourself these questions. Do not *FEAR* (False Evidence Appearing Real). We have all the answers within us. Ask your *SELF* and you shall receive the answers.

The importance of present moment is that you are in Spirit. You sit in your Divine seat. You are connected to your birthright, a Divine soul. In present moment, your Spirit masters your Ego. Mastering who you are and your purpose in this world is so important. If you do not nurture and water your own seed, it will not grow healthy.

When you feel purity, you see through the eyes of the Divine. Divine love and purity can only be lived and felt in present moment. This is pure Spirit. It's unconditional. Ego has you in war with yourself. Then you want to go to war with others. What is within you also lives outside of you. In Ego, you judge, you make false assumptions; you make poor and unhealthy agreements for yourself and with others.

We are a world of relationships. We mirror each other. This is how we see ourselves when we cannot look in our own mirror. It's hard to take a good look at yourself because the first thing you will do is judge yourself. And if you do not like yourself, you become the victim under your Judge character. You will label just about everything. Labeling is creating false identity. Have you ever heard the saying, "you are your worst critic"? You are! You will judge YOU and reflect it in others. This is not being in present moment. This is ego and acting out your role in the Book of Laws.

There comes a time that you will look at your agreements you have made with others and life. This is not judgment. This is what I call "clearing out" and making "healthy changes" along the way. It's an understanding of who you are and the justifications whether your thoughts or actions have been healthy for you or not. This is part of the dis-creation process. You can't clear your mind-slate unless you are present.

When you are in present moment, you will be able to see all clearly, feel what feels good and what does not. You will feel through practice what feels blissful to you. Your solar plexus will reflect happiness or anxiety. The solar plexus is the seat of your emotions and has a mental memory stored in your physical body. Not necessarily all you feel in your solar plexus is in present moment. The solar plexus carries past memories also. If you feel the slightest edge on decisions you have made, emotions you have absorbed, then ask yourself, "why am I feeling this within?" Do not judge. That is what the Ego would want you to do, become the Judge you have been most of your life and then you easily fall into the victim role. This role will have you going back and forth between the two. This can be a vicious role to act out and a hard habit to break, but it can be done. You can only eliminate it in present moment.

When visions of the past come to haunt you, let them play out, do not judge. When you make a clear decision for yourself, you are not judging. You are living your belief. Our beliefs can be conditioned or unconditional. It is so important that you remain in gratitude because it will keep you present and not let your Ego master your Spirit. Your thoughts will create your day. Why not empower your thoughts in gratitude and create the day?

Complaining is an avoidance of you taking action

I touched briefly on complaining earlier in this book. When we complain, we block energy to create. When we complain about our life, worries, success, work, family, and relationships, we can't appreciate all we have achieved. When we complain about our relationships, we continue to find more issues with our relationships. When we complain about our health, our health concerns and illnesses increase. When we complain about our debts, monies, stress, failures, the more we attract in the same issues and the stronger they become. Silence yourself and go beyond these complaints. Look and feel why you have created and became these worldly issues. They were not handed to you; somewhere in your thought process you created them. You were taught by your caretakers or friends at an early age on how to complain. When we feel the worldly pressures of debts and heartbreaks, we get caught up in the greed and not the gratitude.

Our Emotional Connections

I want to say this is probably one of the most important factors. Our emotions play a great part in our creation. If we are sad and stay with sadness, we attract more sadness. If we are happy and try our best to be grateful, we become more at bliss. When we love unconditionally, we receive love from all avenues and unconditionally. When we love conditionally, we place barriers and restrictions upon love and it can only attract in restricted love. When we hate life or people, we create more people and things to hate in life. You can choose how to live your life. Choosing to be beautiful emotionally within can create such love in your life.

There are ups and downs in life. Keeping a positive attitude, feeling grateful for all that you have and experienced will help greatly in balancing your emotional body. Allow your emotions to be free in gratitude.

The world is the way it is and we should be grateful

That's right. You are not the world. You are a spiritual being in a physical body having both a spiritual and a physical experience. You are not your body nor are you the world. When we carry the world upon our shoulders, we begin to create illusions. Your inner world, the Divine Being and Light you are is your true essence. Be grateful for experiencing your life in this world but don't become the world. Share your beauty and your unconditional love by sending out love to the world in the form of Divine blessings. The world around you is the dyad of worldly thought processes. By sending good positive thoughts to the world will help the world become a better humane place to live. Be grateful for your breath as a contribution only in love, light, peace and *BEING* (Divine).

Believe in miracles, you will attract miracles

If you believe in miracles, and believe with all the gratitude you have in your heart, you will be heard by your heavenly helpers and miracles can happen. They happen every day. Sometimes we are so down; we have a hard time getting up. This is when we say- I am grateful with much gratitude and abundance that I am having a miracle experience. By saying you are having a miracle experience, you will attract in that miracle.

What is a miracle? A miracle is when our Infinite Helpers aid in assisting you in what you want. Whether it is Divine, Goddess, Angels, Spirit Guides, or Ancestry Warriors, they are available to assist us in our daily needs. I can share many stories of Infinite assistance.

One time I was greatly despaired. I was talking to a girlfriend over the phone and I didn't know what to do. I was feeling down, a bit lost and unloved. I was working in my own pet care business and had driven to the place where I was to care for a client's pet. I got out of the car, while still complaining to my girlfriend and walked across the street. A man approached with two bundles of flowers in his hand. He walked past me and I followed. Suddenly, he turned around and looked at me with this blank look on his face. "These are for you," he said without even a mere smile on his face. I was surprised. I could feel a shiver of delight come over me. I said, "thank you," with much gratitude. He turned away and walked toward a building where I presumed he either lived or was visiting. I felt the presence of an Angel and that Angel worked through this man and the gift of flowers really made me feel special and picked up my spirit and I felt loved. So you see miracles happen in many ways.

Find what's good and make that your reality

Don't fret about the negative. Again, like attracts like. Seek and you shall find. Ask and you shall receive. *BELIEVE.* Look for all the good, even if more seems bad than good. You will find that one thread of goodness can stretch beyond the horizons. I can't even tell you what a blessing this is once you discover it. Stay with it; don't let the negative pins and needles that have been sticking you daily continue to stress you. Know and trust that gratitude is a magical blessing and merge her however you can into your life.

By focusing on what is good for you, you attract in more good. By focusing on the light side of things, you attract more light. Focus is another word for intent. We can meditate and intend good for us or others. We can walk-meditate through nature and intend good for us or we can just sit and intend. Be conscious of what you are intending. Be as clear and focused as you possibly can.

Being gratitude through Smile and Laughter

They say that laughter is the best medicine for the soul. It is! The more you smile, the more you bring smiles to others. The gift in return is feeling bliss in your life. The more you laugh, the happier you are and this alone will bring more laughter and love in your life. Laughing in gratitude brings more laughter and smiles in your life. The sun shines internally. Look at all the happy faces in others you will create by smiling and laughing as much as you can. Gratitude will make you feel this way.

What is PAIN?

Pain is P=Past, A=Attitudes and Assumptions, I=In Ignorant bliss, N=Not Present. How can we heal PAIN? P=Please, A=Accept, I=Infinite Blessings, N=NOW. We feel pained when we are consistently reviewing past memories that have caused us pain. The memory will consistently remind us of this deep feeling until we accept what has happened, happened. We can't change what happened but we can change our behavior toward the lesson. You need to understand that the past needs to remain in the past. Gratitude can help assist us that whatever occurred was experienced for the evolution of our soul. Current pain needs to be felt and expressed before it builds up anger. It's ok if you feel anger as anger can help heal the pain if it's expressed constructively. Also anger that remains stagnant within us is not healthy and can create more negative energy. By accepting what happened, happened gives a sense of relief because it brings you into present moment. All of us have been hurt one time or another in life. The only way we are going to move forward from this pain is to be thankful in gratitude that we survived through it and that we have learned from our experience. When we are grateful for the experience, the painful experience becomes a lesson of gratitude. Try it and you will see what I mean.

We remember the experience more so in PAIN than we do in a *BLISSFUL* moment because PAIN is like a Disease (Dis-Ease) and Bliss is healing! So why do so many of us experience PAIN? Because we are living in Ego which tells us that all that has happened is still happening. But it's not. It's just an illusion to fool you into not *BEING* (BE-IN-GOD-SELF) and awakened within you. When we are not awakened consciously, we are sleeping unconscious *BEINGS*. Being unconscious means we are not living our birthright-*BEING*.

Loving unconditionally

Professor Mario Beauregard, from Montreal University's center for research into neurophysiology and cognition, used MRI to study active areas of the brain of people, who were most likely to experience unconditional love. Subjects were asked to call to mind feelings of unconditional love. Researches saw 7 active areas in the brain. Three of those areas were similar to regions in the brain that became active when it came to romantic love. The other four were different, which means that the feeling of love for someone without the need of being rewarded is different from the feeling of romantic love.

In his study, Professor Beauregard found that some brain areas that turned on when a person felt unconditional love also engaged in discharging dopamine, chemical that plays a role in sensing pleasure.

Studies and research by Harold W. Becker, author and founder of (nonprofit) The Love Foundation, Inc., led to a practical contemporary definition stating that, "unconditional love is an unlimited way of being." Experienced within the individual, this universal awareness of love operates on every level of life through the physical, emotional, mental and spiritual bodies and is expressed when one becomes conscious of its presence. This is true love. We can begin to feel this true love through gratitude.

Letting go of judgment

"Out beyond ideas of wrong doing, and right doing, there is a field. I will meet you there".

RUMI

26

We judge because we are taught to judge. We label things and people because we were taught this (*The Book of Laws*). Rather than thinking about what our own needs are, we place blame on others when they don't meet our needs. Even before we were born, before entering this world, we have chosen the road to judge. We also judge because we're in the habit of judging. But when all is said and done, our judgments only reflect ourselves, not others.

"When you judge another, you do not define them, you define yourself."

WAYNE DYER

Dr. Marshall Rosenberg, author of *Non-violent Communication: A Language of Life,* says that, "certain ways of communicating alienate us from our natural state of compassion."

The first "life-alienating" form of communication is moralistic judgment. Moralistic judgment implies wrongness or badness on the part of someone who doesn't act in accord with our own values.

Sometimes we get angry just because someone doesn't fit in with our sense of morals and values. It could be "habit energy," as Thich Nhat Hanh calls it in *Anger: Wisdom for Cooling the Flames.* It could be something we learned from our parents or friends, and through this conditioning we judge race, sex, and creed. We may find fault in others because we are hurt and we expect a certain treatment or behavior from someone and we don't know how else to express this or how to handle it. Finding fault with others can be habitual.

Another way of judging is when someone doesn't fit in the categories we create. We may not like the way they act, what they speak, how they treat us and the list can go on. We will continue to judge others until we accept others as they are. In acceptance, you will know if this person can be a part of your life or not. We even judge our animals. We judge them when they may make an accident in the house. When we accept to change our behavior, then we accept to change within. So this happens with all of us, including the animal who attends behavioral training. Gratitude helps us to eliminate judgment.

Throw away your human book of knowledge. We say, "I know that already." If we say, "I know that already," then how come we are not applying it? We all have gut feelings. Our gut feelings or intuition is our gift of wisdom. Listen to it. Our intuition doesn't chitter-chatter. Our best sight and wisdom is spent in silence.

The Book of Knowledge is a book that has been passed along generation after generation. It is full of conditions, control, judgment, criticism, jealousy and hypocrisy. It reflects the Ego in us all. These are HUMAN Laws. And we have learned to listen, read and absorb this book as all of our caretakers and friends have recited from it one time or another. We have even added our own laws along the way.

When we understand wisdom, accept the natural flow within us, we are connected to our birthright, a Divine spirit that is working our soul's calling in life. We are in touch with the essence of who we are, and our mission in the world. Don Miguel Luis in his books, "*The Four Agreements*" and "*The Four Agreements Companion*" speaks about the Book of Knowledge or better known as the Book of Laws. *The Book of Knowledge* is also a fantastic book. Everyone should read these.

Change and Choices

Anyone and anything can change. We have the power and that power is our Intent. When we believe something very strongly, we put a lot of energy behind it. This is our Intent. Never say that no one can change. We just can't change someone. People change all the time. People with negative habits awaken and become enlightened. That is change. Our nature changes every season, even our own personal garden. We change our home around, or change places to live. We change cars, clothes, shoes, jewelry, and even relationships. In gratitude, we accept change. Change for the better is always for the higher good.

So how do we change? We change within. When we realize that our outer world reflects who we are within. When we awaken and see the life we have been living. The pain we repetitively keep repeating in our heads, the noise we make outside, the wars we keep fighting, the criticism and the judgments, the lack of applying wisdom, when we awaken to all this, then we want change. When we live our lives in negative ways, we see only what I just mentioned. More negative ways. We cannot change for anyone but ourselves. Who holds the master plan within you? You do. You hold the master plan with the Divine in you. Your master plan is your birthright. It is up to you to re-discover it. To return within to the forces you were born with. When we look in our own mirror and see who we are, then we can say we are awakened. In gratitude you will see what a lovely soul you are and you will want to be the change. That change is *BEING* your birthright.

We can choose to do anything we like. We have the power and that power is our Intent. Are we choosing just to choose? Do we know what we want to choose? Are we awakened enough to feel the difference between choices? Are we choosing to fit the lack, or are we choosing to fit the gain? Are we choosing to be the LIGHT or are we choosing to be the DARK? Are we choosing to fully live our SPIRIT, or are we choosing to live our EGO? Are we choosing to live the outside world for others or are we choosing to begin within our own temple and reflect out? We give gratitude and love with a pure heart, but we do not breathe for another. We encourage another to breathe for their own love and light, so that they may also give unconditionally.

Gratitude and respect

Your W.E.A.L.T.H. is your relationship with other people. What is WEALTH? Most would compare or label WEALTH with money and material possession. Am I right? But WEALTH is Divine and has to do what you are wealthy in. For example, I am wealthy with great health. W=Wake up. Wake up and enlighten! E=Enthusiasm. This is the Divine within us, giving us direction and inspiration. A=Angels. Acceptance, abundance, inspiring ideas, messages and Light. L=Love. Love is the wealthiest light we can ever give and receive. Without love, we are not light. Without our Sun to shine it's Light on all living things, we eventually die. Every living thing would die. T=Thank you with much gratitude and abundance. H-Help yourself first. If you can't help yourself first you cannot truly help another. When you live WEALTH within, you become WEALTH and it reflects outwardly in your world.

Relax, meditate, be stress free

Relaxation is important. You can learn to relax through meditation. There are many self hypnosis CD's to help you learn how to relax and meditate. You can go and visit a hypnotist or someone educated in meditation and relaxation. Yoga, Tai Chi, Qigong are very good programs that include meditation and relaxation. There are many individual meditation classes that teach all levels of meditation and mind power to relax and let go.

Stress is the number one killer. It produces all types of illnesses and it begins within us. Stress is one way we hold on to conditions and habits. Our organs, cellular and nervous system suffer under stress. Our chakras become so overloaded that this overflows into our aura. It is not the outer that is the cause of this congestion but our inner being that is not aligned due to stress. One of the leading mental causes of stress is trust. When we do not trust, this causes a great deal of stress within us. When we do not love unconditionally, this also causes a great resistance within us. To love conditionally is not our birthright. It has been taught by us through our parents and friends. When we are grateful for whom we are, grateful for all we have, grateful to feel love and to be loved, then we become whole, balanced and peaceful.

The Power of Unconditional Love is to know that you are loved. You are loved unconditionally by our Creator. The Divine's Sacred Love is most powerful within. If you do not know how to believe in this then understand that there is a part of you that loves YOU. This part of you that loves you is the birthright of you and the Divine seat within. You are connected to Creator. There is no judging, competition, or any reason other than that you are loved within and so therefore you are this unconditional love. You are being loved just as you are.

Unconditional love is beyond a conditional and physical love. You are loved beyond reasons or any purpose, you are loved beyond judgment and imperfections, and you are loved beyond any word or action. You are eternally you and loved unconditionally.

Beginning the "Gratitude" path

Below is a "sample list" to help you focus on the road to gratitude. We all have experienced this form of gratitude in some way. You may have experienced this at a sermon in church, Sunday school lessons, meditation class, or just someone who had the experience of the magic of gratitude and shared it with you. Either way, this is a very good beginning. Most of us have been taught to say thank you, give, and pray for blessings. It was taught to us with knowledge that we would benefit from giving thanks by receiving blessings from the Divine.

But how many of us have really felt the energy of gratitude? Most of us just touch the mere tip of it by saying "thank you", "God Bless You", and "I'll pray for you." By exploring and absorbing gratitude, sharing it amongst others, you will receive much happiness. Abundance will be yours. It is the *KEY* that awakens the Law of Attraction.

Most people understand the gratitude in some way or form. But how many give and receive gratitude in their lives daily? Below is a list that you can begin to focus on and give much, much gratitude. First, give the gratitude and thanks to the Divine. Second, thank your Angels and Guides that walk with you or assist in answering your prayers. They are Divine blessed and a part of the Immaculate Universe.

- **Your health.** Be grateful for your health. If it is not in the best state, be grateful also so that you can assist in changing the direction of the winds and bring in gratitude to your health conditions.
- **Your house.** Be grateful for having a roof over your head. Look at the bright side of all you did to create this home.
- **The clothes on your back.** Be grateful for all the clothes you wear. It is not important the value of your clothes in currency but rather how blessed you are to have clothes on your back.
- **Your possessions**. Look at all you have gained. Bless all your possessions. Be grateful that you were able to obtain all of your possessions.
- **Your relationships**. Feel blessed in gratitude for all your relationships.
- **Your family**. Feel blessed in gratitude for all the family you have today.
- **Your job**. Be grateful for your job, career or profession. Look at your skills with greatness on what you have been able to create and establish for yourself. If you are jobless at this time, be grateful for your dreams that you will find one. Be grateful for all you once had and that better things are coming, NOW.
- **Your skills.** It is always a blessing to be grateful for all the skills you have acquired. These are your gifts to share with others. Be grateful

for them and all the lessons, schooling that you had acquired to develop these skills. Go deeper and feel these skills. Connect any skill that makes you feel good and visualize how much of your skill is connected to your Divine birthright.

- **The moments you have in life.** Always be grateful for any moment of life. Whether happy or sad, your moments in life are worth more than anything else in this world. Cherish your life as it was given to you by our Great Creator.

"Gratitude unlocks the fullness of life. It turns what we have into enough, and more. It turns denial into acceptance, chaos to order, confusion to clarity. It can turn a meal into a feast, a house into a home, a stranger into a friend. Gratitude makes sense of our past, brings peace for today, and creates a vision for tomorrow."

MELODY BEATTIE

Gratitude keeps growing and beyond. This is living your life in Bliss

In time, gratitude keeps growing within you and even beyond. It's magical! I like to call it "gratitude that seeds the bliss" because it involves being grateful for spiritual and universal laws. The Universe is made of the gratitude structure. We overlook this a lot! The Law of Attraction works magically here because we are independent of worldly situations and circumstances. In other words, we are living in the world, but we are not of it. We believe we are well taken care of. We trust gratitude and all she blesses us with. This eliminates stress, worrying, and any other negative habitual condition. Gratitude is the most effective way to practice the Law of Attraction. When we practice gratitude, magic happens. Gratitude is everything bliss. Within gratitude are Divine blessings. The more you practice it, the more it merges with you. There is no need to separate gratitude. It should be included in everything you do, see, taste, and hear. Gratitude is *WHOLE*.

Do you feel that you deserve bliss? Most people do not. Many suffer from low self esteem. They believe that they deserve suffering. They will not admit it. They are not conscious of it. When you say to yourself, I deserve gratitude; you immediately feel a sense of power. But then you have your adversary to deal with and in return will talk you out of feeling gratitude. It will talk you into what you have only experienced. You can change this. It only takes being responsible in wanting to be grateful. It's important that when you walk the walk of gratitude, you devote yourself to it.

As you go through the list below and feel grateful for all you have, you will begin to feel your life as uplifted and feel happier every day. That is, if you continuously practice. It will become a part of you. You will feel the difference on what your Ego has been producing all along and what a difference it is to be just in Spirit. How good it feels to feel good! How gratitude will bring you quickly into acceptance.

- **Your life.** Be grateful that you have a life. Even if it is not the best life, if you want to change the vibrations of it, you must be grateful for your life.
- **The Universe.** We are grateful with much gratitude and abundance for the Universe. Our Universe supports our living. Let us be grateful for life and the Universe.
- **Time and Space.** We are grateful for time. There is no time on the Spiritual Plane but there is on Earth. This has a lot to do with our lessons we chose to learn along the way. The more we are grateful for our time and accept our life in gratitude, time become less important. Our space is important as this is our circle of sacredness. Find a place where you can give time in your Sacred Space where you can meditate and sit with gratitude. All the Laws occupy space within our minds.
- **Your problems.** I know this one can be a difficult one, as bills, debts all begin to pile up. The more you become your problems, the less manageable they become and the more problems you will attract in. Be grateful for all that you have been able to maintain by not complaining and in gratitude you will be able to see what you have been lacking that caused these problems to flourish.

- **Your imperfection.** We are not perfect. The only perfection you want to achieve is *BEING* in your Divine seat, your birthright and living within your blueprint.
- **Your mistakes.** We all make them and there is no right or wrong. What has occurred is a life experience for the advancement of your soul. Be grateful for mistakes. They are great lessons.
- **Friends and Enemies.** Be grateful for your friends. True friends are hard to come by and they should be treated with much gratitude. Your enemies are your best teachers. Be grateful for them as they are only enemies of your Ego and through gratitude you will learn that most your outlook regarding who you have labeled as enemy is an illusion. Your position in gratitude will change your enemies to friends or they will be removed entirely. Remember the more you look at something negative, the more negative it becomes. We should all have boundaries to protect ourselves from being a victim to a weak soul. The boundaries are not for the other, but for you. Somewhere within you, you are not sure of your higher self and therefore are weak in the trust. By making boundaries, you are agreeing with your higher self regarding what is good for you or not. Let go and trust. What is not good for your higher self will be eliminated. As you journey with gratitude, the Ego will not want to protect as much because your Spirit will flourish blissfully and Master all that you fear and judge.

Both abundance and lack exist simultaneously in our lives, as parallel realities. It is always our conscious choice which secret garden we will tend... when we choose not to focus on what is missing from our lives but are grateful for the abundance that's present – love, health, family, friends, work, the joys of nature and personal pursuits that bring us pleasure – the wasteland of illusion falls away and we experience Heaven on earth. Sarah Ban Breathnach

Here are some basic guidelines

Create your "sacred" space. This is your inner circle of light. Always find the sacred space or sacred garden within you first. From there, find a space somewhere in your home or out in nature.

Create a gratitude altar. You can place an altar in some private area of your home or even around your sacred space. Place things that represent what you are grateful for, such as photos of people who have been an inspiration in your life. If you love nature, in which I certainly do as I am so grateful we have this beautiful manifestation of love, light, even oxygen from nature.

Without nature, we would not be living on this planet as plants give off oxygen. One of the purposes it was created by our Divine source.

You can place photos or even real pieces of nature, such as trees, plants, flowers, stones, soil, and more. To represent a tree, you can use a branch or leaves, or have a plant that represents a tree and place it by your altar. You can call this altar, your sacred garden. You can add photos of birds or collect figurines in many forms that will assist you on your magical journey with gratitude. You can put up any photo you like that represents spiritual gratitude. It's all in the attitude you empower. You can even take something off your altar daily and carry it with you to remind you of gratitude.

Create a gratitude collage. Another way that will help you visualize gratitude is creating a collage. A collage is a collection of magazine, newspaper, words or anything that you can paste onto a board and create a collage that will speak the magic of gratitude to you.

The "Sacred" Gratitude Journal. A gratitude journal is simply a diary except you record what you are grateful for that day. You could use a diary or similar book for writing your gratitude journal. Just make sure you have enough pages to cover a year's worth of gratitude. Start your journal with the following line – "Today I am grateful for…"Everyday write down 5 things you are grateful for. Now, these things that you have been grateful for during the day could be as simple as being able to eat your breakfast in the morning, being able to read the newspaper. You can also be grateful for the house you live in, having a supportive partner and family that are always there for you.

Even when you are not having a good day, things are not going smoothly, you must still write down your 5 things you have been grateful for during the day. This is where gratitude is most important. You are training yourself though this exercise to go beyond the everyday situations and circumstances in the world. On a side note, you can write the negative things that happened as there are great lessons in doing this. You can see possibly why you had negative vibrations in your life today and what you can do to change it. I accept the negative energy as I am grateful that they are only temporary and that better things are coming in my life, NOW. Doing this exercise will help you to look for things to be grateful for and appreciate them. This will help you create an attitude of gratitude.

In every situation, look for the good things. They are there; you just have to see them. Look for the positive things even when they don't seem to be there. You just have to look for them. Stop complaining and start to think positive. When you are having a really good day, everything just seems to be helping you create an attitude of gratitude; you will have more than 5 things to write in your journal. You can write down everything.

Every day you can be grateful for something. When you tell someone in your life you are grateful for them is a powerful way to express gratitude. Expressing gratitude towards someone who has provided a cheerful smile, given good service or maybe provided you with directions are blissful for all of you.

Ways we can express gratitude could be as simple as sending a card, email or letter thanking someone. Include what it was that made you grateful, how you felt when they made you grateful.

Here is a sample from my own gratitude journal –

"Today I am grateful for wakening to the morning sun. I am grateful to be able to open my eyes, and see such great Light. I am grateful for being able to eat. I am grateful for my car and that I have transportation available to get around. I tell my car how grateful I am for her. I am grateful for being healthy, for having two functional legs and arms, a heart to feel, a mind to create, and all my body parts, both internally and externally are functioning correctly."

This is just a sample of my many daily gratitude entries I have in my journal. It is also important to read through your previous entries and reflect on why you have been grateful. Just remember to write in your journal 5 things that you are grateful for everyday, even when you don't feel like writing.

CHAPTER FIVE

Gratitude Exercises

Exercise 1:

- Choose any room and stand in the center of the room.
- Feel calm, peaceful and relaxed.
- Take a look around the room and move toward the first object that you see.
- Aim to cover every object in the room including furniture, walls, carpets and even the pictures on the walls.
- Say thanks to the object for its usefulness in your life.
- Touch each object or if you can hold the object, pick it up.
- Continue around the room thanking every object for its usefulness in your life.
- Continue with the other rooms and do the same.
- Notice how you feel as you thank each object.
- Return to the center of the first room when finished.
- If you have a lot of objects, don't worry about finishing them in a day. Do what you can.

- Do not go beyond your limitations. If you feel tired, better to leave it for later or tomorrow.

Exercise 2:

- Move around the room again but this time show as much appreciation as you can for the object being in your life.
- Notice how you feel as you thank each object.
- As you go around, appreciate the beauty of the object, how nice it is, how it looks in your home.
- Continue around each room.

Exercise 3:

- Start in the first room.
- Feel calm, peaceful and relaxed.
- When you approach each object, recall everyone that was responsible for its creation and bringing the object to you. Even though you may not know who they all are, say thank you to all those people involved in creating and delivering the object.
- Feel a real sense of gratitude for all those people responsible.
- The earth provided the materials for creating your beautiful object; think how the earth provided the materials for your object.
- Thank the earth with gratitude for providing the raw materials for everything you have.

Exercise 4:

- Return to the first room.
- Feel calm, peaceful and relaxed.
- As you go around the room and approach each object, and imagine what it would be without the object if you could not replace it.
- Imagine how different your life would be without the object.

- How would you feel about losing the object and not being to replace it?
- Experience the feeling of losing the object fully.

Exercise 5:

- Picture everything as being connected to everything else in the world.
- Everything is connected in some shape of form, no one is alone and we depend on being connected with each other to make our lives easier and provide us with things to enjoy life.

The purpose of these exercises is to ground and connect you with the earth, and all living creatures on earth. When doing these exercises, appreciate all living creatures and be impartial to color, age, race, shape and size and also gender.

Exercise 6:

- Make sure you are warm and find somewhere comfortable to sit.
- Feel calm, peaceful and relaxed.
- If you wish to write things down, have a pen and paper handy.
- You can either make a mental note or write it down as a prompt.
- Recall all the people you have had contact with in your life. This will include your parents and family, extended family and anyone else including friends and enemies, your teachers, customers and anyone else you have met or had contact with in your life.
- Your list should be very long.
- Thank everyone for being in your life at one time or another.
- All these people have shaped you into being who you are today.

Exercise 7:

- Now work though the same list of people and appreciate their assisting in your life.

- Don't forget to appreciate the people, who have caused you discomfort, anger and hurt, etc, they have also been a part of your life.
- These people are teaching you lessons, even if you don't agree with what they are teaching you. This is a great lesson on how we should treat others.
- Now appreciate the people who have helped you along the way in your life.
- Stay focused and do not let past feelings enter and judge anyone. Focus on the ways people have shaped your life.

Exercise 8:

- Feel calm, peaceful and relaxed.
- Now work through your list, thanking all the people for their energy and the many experiences, either good or not so good you had with them.
- Have a feeling of gratitude towards everyone on your list.
- All these people have helped shape your life, into what it is today, they have helped you make decisions, be independent, provide love and hate.

Exercise 9:

- Feel calm, peaceful and relaxed.
- Now work through your list, and imagine if you had never had met these people, how different your life would be.
- You may not know how different your life would have been without these people, either good or not good.
- How do you feel towards a particular person?
- If these people were not in your life, would you have any regrets or would you be pleased?
- Would you have gone down a different path without these peoples' influence on your life?

- What experiences would not have occurred if these people were not there to lend you a hand and guide you through life?
- Would you feel good or not so good if these people had not been there?
- Now give gratitude to all these people for being in your life, either good or not so good.

Exercise 10:

- Now picture how each person has played a part in your life.
- This time think about the part you have played in other people's lives.
- Maybe you have caused them to be joyful, brought laugher to them, provided assistance to them or had similar effects.

Would the people you have had contact with, regret or rejoice if you had not been in their lives? If you have never met these people would their lives have been the same? Now send each person you have ever had contact with gratitude, appreciation, and love for experiencing your life.

The Power of Giving Gratitude

When was the last time you gave something because the other person did something to make your day? Did you give because you had to, or did you give because you were grateful for what they did for you? And did you give expecting something in return? When we give we are sending out signals to the universe to attract what we give out. If we give and don't expect anything in return, this activates the Reciprocation Law, the give and receive Universal Law.

Don't focus on what you give, but give everything. Give with love and gratitude. You will receive the same in return. If you give away money, you will receive money. If you give love, you will receive love. What we give, we receive and tenfold. Whatever we give out could come back to us from anywhere and anyone. Always give with gratitude.

Gratitude in Business

Businesses have their ways to say they are grateful to their customers. They run sale ads, giving a percentage off on their merchandise. Some companies offer incentives, depending on what they sell. Both way, they give in gratitude and their return is tenfold. This is a win/win situation for the business. It's also good for you as a customer. They are helping a worthy cause and the business is receiving back what they've sent out to be manifested. Like attracts like. Their intention is to sell the merchandise with a percentage off to attract the consumer to purchase. They sell, you purchase. You get an item on sale and they receive a return on their investments plus. They are using the power of gratitude and conscious creation.

As team players at core level, what you create together and what you send out together will come back tenfold. When there is jealousy and competition, fighting and conflict, too much energy is spent creating disharmony. When you are all on the same blissful page, the intent is to succeed. If you spend your time judging your co-worker, then you are missing moments in production. By being grateful as a team, your energies together create bliss. The more bliss that is created in core-harmony, everyone wins. When we create bliss, we receive bliss. When we work together to create the same goals, our finances increase.

CHAPTER SIX

The Magic of Trust

One must trust themselves in order to trust another. It is not important whether or not you can trust the other person. Trust that lives within you will create trust all around you. All you trust and believe in will manifest blissfully.

There are many who do not trust, and they attract lack of trust. Remember, your outer world is the reflection of your inner world. It begins within first. Your spiritual being within is your true reality. It is your spiritual energy. There is nothing (no-thing) that can't be manifested. If there is greed, selfishness, conditions and jealousy, then expect to manifest this. What you INTENT is your outcome. If you manifest beautiful things, then you as a light *BEING* will feel the gratuity. It's all in your Intention.

Many of you are concerned that if you trust, you will again be taken advantage of. Many of you feel by trusting, this will allow the non-trusting situation to overrule your trust. It will not.

Trust that you can produce and direct spiritual consciousness, pure thought and commit to the action that are the end results of the manifestation. It feels good to trust yourself. Trust love. By trusting love, all attachments and parasites will fade.

What would happen to you if you trusted all things? You would only attract in more things to trust. What would happen if you didn't put a condition on trust? Then trust would set you free. What would happen if you just trusted trust? Trust would bless you.

We have all encountered something or someone we could not trust. We then allowed it to burden us. Even our caretakers may have passed on trust issues. It could be stored in our DNA. We may have encountered many situations or people we could not trust as that is what they mirrored to us. But they mirrored this to us because within us, we already had an issue with trust. When we become this lack of trust, you will receive nothing (no-thing) to trust. Trust even the ones who can't be trusted. When you say this blessing, even the ones who can't be trusted will learn to trust. This is the mirror to mirror effect. One who is not trustworthy does not trust themselves. We are not lack, we are gain. Gain trust by trusting. Then trust shall be yours.

When we trust what we create, our creation is trusted by the Universe. Then the Universe mirrors us back trust. What we are, we attract in. If you care not to be trust, and then understand, you will not be trusted. If you care to trust and be trusted, then so you will be trusted.

To not trust means FEAR (False Evidence Appearing Real). When we do not trust, it gives us control. Control over FEAR. FEAR has no trust because FEAR only knows what it can destroy. FEAR destroys love, bliss and happiness. FEAR gives you more FEAR. Lack of trust, is FEAR. FEAR you will be taken advantage of and used for your natural abilities. Your natural abilities are LOVE and TRUST. FEAR wants you to believe that TRUST will destroy you. FEAR wants you to believe that to trust another in love and truth will only make you a FOOL. This understanding is false and a conditioning of Ego. This is an experience you never healed. FEAR has led you to believe that it is wrong to trust because trust has failed you one time or another. Let go! Love and trust yourself. This is all that is needed to be FREE from FEAR. Be ALL possibilities.

CHAPTER SEVEN

The Levels of the Mind

I want to touch on the different levels of the mind. It is just for your clarification and understanding.

The *subconscious mind* is our best friend and servant. It will do whatever you ask it to do. There are no limits except the ones we place on it and ourselves. It stores our belief system and it will do whatever it can to make that belief a reality. When it comes to thoughts and feelings, it does not discriminate. It will respond to loving thoughts and also fearful thoughts. It will respond to whatever you desire or imagine, so practicing awareness of your thoughts. The subconscious hears all and responds to what it hears. It plays the servant role and sees you as its master.

Our subconscious mind never judges any of our thoughts, feelings or actions. It will not criticize, analyze and is our best friend. It is our conscious mind that analyzes, criticizes and judges and the subconscious mind will listen and obey. Whatever belief system is adapted by the conscious mind, your subconscious friend will adhere. It will also remind you of your painful experiences as it protects you. It is up to you to heal these repressed painful memories.

The subconscious is the home where the heart lies. The heart and subconscious have a link to each other. Your emotions from love to fear are recorded and stored here. It's the memorizing software of every experience encoded (past lives) or programmed from conscious experiences. It also travels down to the cellular structure of our bodies. So if there is a similar event that has happened, the body will also experience it. This is called trigger or trigger points. The thoughts and beliefs we have created regarding similar events also show up instantly.

Now here is the importance of the emotional strength of the subconscious mind. The emotional strength of our love or fear held in our subconscious minds will almost always override rational thoughts coming from our conscious minds. When it comes to a battle of the minds, the subconscious mind will almost always win out. The key to having success in creating what we desire is to convince the subconscious mind to go along with the decisions our conscious mind makes for us. And this is where dis-creating and re-creating is powerful.

The subconscious is the creative, imaginative part of our mind. And the power of the imagination is limitless. Anything we can conceive or imagine can come into being. Imagination is the seed we plant and from there it is watered and grows. The power of the imagination is tenfold. But here is the downfall. If we all our imagination to be controlled by fear, the results can be disastrous. What we imagine can become into BEING. It will work hard to create the negative imagery as well as positive, it just depends on you whether or not you become aware and reprogram. Your subconscious mind depends on your BELIEFS. The good news is your subconscious mind can be re-programmed.

The subconscious is also the universe within. There is an impeccable connection. It's called higher consciousness. And all wisdom is available here. We are always connected with the creator here. When we pray, we reach our subconscious mind. To reach the highest state of mind, you must be silent. You must be beyond the state of consciousness and what most call the Alpha state. You must be in the state of BEING which subconscious mind is present. In this state of BEING, we can access all answers to our questions.

Your subconscious mind records all events. This is your field of awareness. Memories, thoughts and feelings, recordings, belief system and your subconscious mind will bring it to you in any relevant situation. All our thoughts are stored here. We can recall any memory we choose. We can access the Akashic records (recordings of past life experience up until the moment). This is where we will be working to change some of those negative recordings or memories.

The subconscious mind is like the messenger. When we become BEING, we can access our subconscious and create any desire we want. Doesn't matter what level you are in subconsciously. But the best level is to be beyond conscious state in silence. A quiet mind is always a blessing. This is the Alpha state. You can access even deeper, the theta state. The subconscious mind never sleeps. It goes 24/7. So anytime you want to re-program, you can. When we become silent, there is a channel of communication between the conscious, subconscious, and creation. Not only do we communicate from the conscious to the subconscious to creation, but the reverse is also true. Intuition is comes through creation to the subconscious mind and into the conscious mind. All of us have intuition or gut feelings.

Intuition and imagination originate in the creative level of the mind and appear through awareness at conscious level. Conscious creators must understand the relationship between the conscious, subconscious and the creative level. If you want to be the best healer, you will understand that your creative level feeds into your subconscious mind, become higher mind and then proceeds through conscious mind.

The Super Conscious mind has also been called the "universal subconscious mind" and the "collective unconscious." The great Swiss psychoanalyst, Carl Jung, referred to this as the "super conscious mind." He felt that the collective wisdom and knowledge of all the ages was contained in this super conscious mind and was available to everyone.

Ralph Waldo Emerson referred to it as the "over soul" and wrote that, "We live in the lap of an immense intelligence that, when we are in its presence, we realize that it is far beyond our human mind." Emerson, the great American transcendentalist, felt that all power and possibility for the average person came from using this mind on a regular basis.

Thomas Edison used his super conscious mind regularly to come up with hundreds of brand new ideas and inventions, more than 1,000 of which completely transformed America at the beginning of the 20th century. More recently, William Gates came up with an idea for a basic operating system for the early computers, which he called "MS-DOS." It was so unique and revolutionary that he and Paul Allen were actually writing the program on the airplane as they flew to their meeting with their first customer. Today, Bill Gates is the world's richest man, and it all came from a super conscious flash of insight. Bach, Beethoven and Brahms tapped into the super conscious mind regularly to write some of the finest music ever heard. Mozart was so finely tuned into his super conscious mind that he could both see and hear the music in his head and was then able to write down some of the most beautiful music of the ages, note perfect, the very first time he put pen to paper.

Because of your super conscious powers, anything that you can hold in your mind on a continuing basis, you can have. Emerson wrote, "A man becomes what he thinks about, most of the time." Earl Nightingale wrote, "You become what you think about." Of course, there is a potential danger in the use of your super conscious mind. It is like fire. It can be a wonderful servant, but a terrible master. If you use it improperly, and think negative, fearful thoughts, your super conscious mind will accept your thoughts as a command and go to work to materialize them into your reality. What is the difference between successful people and unsuccessful people? It is as simple as this: Successful people think and talk about what they want, and unsuccessful people talk about what they don't want.

The Unconscious Mind is the part of the mind that controls your body functions, such as breathing, immunity, heartbeat and so on. The functions we never pay attention too and just seem to run on their own. This part of the mind is the most mysterious to us, as we know very little about it. The unconscious mind does everything below our awareness. And sometimes we do things that we are not aware of or have a clue why we did it in the first place.

The Conscious Mind is the thinker, the logical and analytical part of your mind. It's the part of the mind that must give you a reason for why you do what you do. Your conscious mind also deals with your willpower and temporary memory. Your conscious mind is what you use most of the time. Well, as far as having an actual knowledge of using it. The conscious mind is very important to us because without it we would be useless. No one could make decisions; make judgments or figure things out.

Your conscious mind can switch from one thought to another within a split second. Always pulling the information you need from another part of the mind. This part of our mind can hold us back as it always has to give a reason for everything we do. Everything has to make sense to this part of the mind.

For instance, have you ever tried to quit smoking before or lose a little weight? Well the moment you start giving yourself positive suggestions such as I'm a non-smoker or I'm losing weight everyday this part of the mind kicks in and rejects it. Why? Because it looks for past experiences and beliefs that match with your new suggestions and if it can't find any it rejects them. Why? Because to this part of the mind how can you 'be' a non-smoker when you smoked yesterday? It has to do things logical and have a reason for everything.

So since this suggestion is rejected. Your chances of becoming a non-smoker have gone down big time. Now, once in a while some suggestions will slip through the natural defense of the conscious mind, which we will call the critical factor. The critical factor is basically the guard at the gate.

It is the part of the conscious mind that determines if the new suggestions match current beliefs. If they don't the gate stays closed and nothing gets in.

CHAPTER EIGHT

Affirmations alone are not enough to create a blissful life

Affirmations are good place to start but they are not enough. Your mind is the carrier of thousands of negative thoughts compared to maybe a thousand positive ones. The older you get, the more negative thoughts accumulate, attached also to one another. In order to get into accordance of your birthright, you will need to dis-create one negative thought at a time. One negative memory will have many attachments to it. When you dis-create an attachment one by one, you will get to the core of the source. The results are amazing!

When you begin the path to really wanting to live a healthy and thought-ful life, you must work on your behavioral thought patterns. Many do not understand that the reason their life is the way it is, is because it began within the mind, the thinking-software. Once you reprogram the software, and use the power of positive thought creation, you will begin to see change in your life for the better.

Your Divine thought software is capable of changing your life instantly. I have taught you the base of gratitude. Get creative with gratitude. You know when gratitude is working because there will be a natural smile to your face. Your life will begin to flourish. You feel good. You want to share this gratitude with everyone and anything. You can't help but to smile with gratitude.

Gratitude opens doors automatically for a greater opportunity. One may think, "how can I be grateful to the Universe or even within me when I have lost my job, lost my house and I am a victim of the economy and my marriage or relationship is over?" Friends and family say move on after a divorce or a break-up. You are moving on regardless of your personal situation. But are you moving in the direction that gives you bliss? Are you repeating negative behavior patterns? Are you remaining stagnant and life's experiences just keep repeating themselves?

You can change your world by being conscious of your thoughts and actions. This changes your world and you are one more soul vibrating in WHOLE. Look around you. What do you see? You hear and read the news, and what do you hear and read mostly? Negative. There are more negative happenings in this world than positive just like what's in your mind. See the correlation? It begins with you to dis-create your Book of Laws, your Judge and the Victim role and consciously create a positive world. You can do it. There are many who achieve this. You just have to BELIEVE!

The power of belief is an amazing or can be the worst gift you can have. The Power of Belief can have you empower or it can have you fear. Empowerment is Light. Fear is dark. FEAR is False Evidence Appearing Real. You can be the empowerment and create positive affirmations as long as you are aware of your negative behavioral patterns within your thoughts and actions. Once you are aware and dis-create the negative pattern, you can really empower from within in a beautiful way, flowing beautiful energy and creating a beautiful dream world. Is there such a thing as perfection? No, but we can perfect our thought patterns and affirm beauty and not ugly. What you send out, you get back in return. What you create, you will experience it. Cause and effect is real. Send out beautiful thoughts and change your Dream World. I believe we are all here for the same purpose and share similar tests. Why not Ace these tests with dis-creating all those old belief patterns and create new and positive ones that bring you your desired results? If you consciously create in a magnitude of great appreciation, eliminate fear and really see your intent for the good, the Universe will resonate all back to you all you have created. There are some hinders though. Whatever you created beforehand, know that it's manifested. You can cancel this hindrance by really focusing on letting go and being that light within you.

I want to discuss your DNA. When you were born, your birthright was pure. You have not been conditioned just yet. As time goes by, the conditioning begins. Please do not take this in a bad way, but honestly our caretakers only followed the guidelines and conditions that were taught to them by their caretakers and the process continues through ancestry. It is not until we become conscious of our thought process and our *BEING* that we can have the power to change our DNA. There are many mechanisms to our minds. We do not use all of them. We even have the power to move objects with just sending thought and energy. Your thoughts have great power. Our beliefs have great power. Now take a look at one of your negative beliefs. Look at how it has kept the fire dwindling in attracting more to your negative belief patterns. Look at that memory power. We have great mental power.

When we do not let go, we create attachments. Those attachments can attach to most of our thoughts. Even if we feel excited and positive over something, watch how it easily burns out and we quickly go downhill. All it takes is one of those attachments to reveal itself through the power of memory and that great belief power takes a hold and off you go into EGO. And if you do not become conscious of these memories that flash periodically in your thought process, it will have you swinging like a pendulum. Generally, we are conditioned to remember the past when we should leave the past where it belongs, in the past.

All parts of our mind work simultaneously. The mind does not work like chapters in a book, and when you are finished thinking, you can put the mind-book down. I included in this book the different levels of mind; it's there for you to understand as you work on your thinking pattern to become a Divine Conscious Creator. Positive affirmations do not work alone. You need to dis-create the demon to re-create the Light. Dis-create Ego and re-create your birthright, a beautiful Divine Spirit. The soul has much to accomplish and it can't do the work it wants to do being a prisoner of the Ego.

Your imagination is a great tool. It is part of the software of visualization that creates the thought-story. Call it day dreaming, call it as you like, but it's your imagination. When you imagine, you are also creating. You are beginning to put the retrospect of visualization and thought into action. A developed and strong imagination does not make you a daydreamer and impractical. On the contrary, it strengthens your creative abilities, and is a great tool for recreating and remodeling your world and life.

This is a great power that can change your whole life. It is used extensively in divine magic, creative visualization and affirmations. It is the creator from circumstances and events. When you know how to work with it, you can make your dream world come true. Imagination has a great role and value in our lives. It is much more than daydreaming. We all use it, whether consciously or unconsciously, daily. We use our imagination whenever we plan a vacation, a meeting, writing a story, how to make grandma's famous apple pie or even giving one directions on how to get from one place to another. What we imagine with a tremendous belief or power comes into being. It is the power beyond creative visualization, positive thinking and affirmations.

That being said, you have begun the dis-creation process, visualizing what you want, and repeating it often in mental image, attracts your desire into your life. This opens up a new, and incredible journey for you. Many doors open and opportunities await you.

Stop the random thinking. Throughout the day, we find ourselves in thought. We do not realize where we go in thought and it's important that you keep tabs on this. Keeping tabs will also show you your thought process and if what you are thinking is negative or positive. This is why present moment is very important because it doesn't contain thinking, but feeling.

Feeling has no judgment, where thinking does. We know we need to think as a take-off to consciously create our desire and goals. Our minds can jump from one thought to another. By working on your thought process, you can dis-create the negative thinking by awareness, and through visualization you can re-create positive thoughts. The more you become aware, the more you will find that what you are thinking is creating your outside environment. We are what we think as it begins within us. So when we complain about our outer life, know that it began within you first. Changing how you live and think within will change your outer environment.

CHAPTER NINE

The Power of the Imagination

This means that we should think only in a positive manner about our desires, otherwise we may create and attract into our lives events, situations and people that we don't really want. This is actually what most of us do, because we don't use the power of imagination correctly. And to use the power of imagination correctly, one must be aware of their negative thoughts and dis-create (clean the slate) and recreate through imagination.

To understand the importance of the power of the imagination, you will create the desired result in your life. If you do not understand it and unconsciously create negative images through your imagination or visualization, your life may not be as happy and successful as you would have wanted it to be. Your life reflects who you are within. When you set the role that consists of pure thought, a powerful and creative imagination and visualization, the outcome is manifestation through the Law of Attraction.

Lack of understanding of the power of the imagination is responsible for the suffering. When your negative thinking patterns merge into your imagination, you have created your suffering. We are conditioned to think failure before success. Why is this? Within our DNA ancestry there may have been suffering and a lack of a powerful-positive-creative imagination. All it takes is one person who can create or dis-create success. One very powerful believer, that can create negative behavioral patterns through the thought and imagination process, can transfer failure and suffering. I know this truth because I grew up in a home as such. Just like one very powerful believer can also create bliss and success. There has been a lot of suffering in this world because our thoughts have created the suffering. When you understand that using your imagination in a conscious creative way, your wisdom is put into action and you can have the pathway to bliss. A creative imagination becomes visualization and the creative seed is planted and grows. Remember, what is above is below and what is below is above.

A story of a young adult who wanted to go to college but the parents said they could not afford it, shared a negative thought process through imagination with their son by showing him he cannot succeed because it will take money to make him succeed and his parents did not have money. Instead of creating the visualization that going to college was their son's dream world, they conditioned him to believe his own creative imagination was powerless. This contains the power of thought, converted into the power of the word and an agreement between the sender and the receiver. I will get into this in another chapter.

Now, there are some very successful entrepreneurs who have created WEALTH from a negative thinker. They did not allow the negative vibration to transfer into them because they believed in the Divine power and their birthright to create anything they imagined and knew ALL possibilities existed.

Now here is the importance of dis-creating negative thoughts. The power of the imagination is very strong. It sets the wheels in motion for visualization which leads to manifestation. If you allow negative memories to consciously or unconsciously surface, you just created through the power of imagination, your movie with unhappy scenes. It's going to play out unless you CANCEL it or become AWARE during the creation process and stop it. This is conscious creation. Conscious creation is performed in the PRESENT MOMENT or NOW stage. You are functioning in Spirit which is your Divine seat or birthright and feeling fresh and pure. You feel within and not without and your beliefs are strong as you can sense through awareness that ALL is exact.

Meditation

Hu Dalconzo, a fabulous conscious creator and Life Coach who created the Holistic Learning Center, shares with his clients and students a Distinctive Meditation that will keep you present and also help you to become aware of your mind and body reactions to thought. Through this meditation, you will become aware of how it feels to be conscious (Spirit) and unconscious (Ego). Spirit is always conscious and aware of its presence where Ego is our lovely negative-adversary and only knows what it has experienced. It's defensive, a protector but can also be a destroyer. I am not saying that Ego is always negative, but most of the time it is because it can and will remind you of a past memory that may or may not have anything to do with your current experience. Spirit sees and feels everything free and for your higher good where Ego will try to protect you, keep you safe and secure in an illusion as it only knows what has happened in the past, not present. Your Ego will also convince you that the story has no ending. It will consistently present a darker side of the imagination and help you to remain in that negative thought and visualization rather than Spirit, forgiving, seeing and feeling what truth is and always for the higher good of your soul. Sometimes the Ego will be correct in protecting you, where you have unconsciously attracted in something that is similar that you had experienced in the past.

Here is an example of someone who consistently attracts in poor relationships. She was abandoned at an early age by her father. She is conditioned to think her father is not a good man. She begins to build on this thought by adding her own personal experiences besides everything that may have been programmed by her caretakers or friends. They proceed to condition her with their own belief process through thought that may not be for her higher good as they may be reflecting their own pain modules to their thought process and passed it along through the word.

We pass our negative as well as our positive thinking along to others whether it is a conscious teaching or not. As she gets older and begins to date, she attracts in her old thinking patterns which are negative and co-dependent. She attracts a man who will match a similar role or identity to her father that abandoned her. She has accepted negative beliefs and built on the process by creating negative thoughts consistently that attached like a magnet to the original negative thought. Now she's run this through her mind on a regular basis because within her she is hurt and abandoned and does not know how to heal herself because she has not been made aware that her thinking is mostly negative. Loving and comforting words can heal a lot. We visualize this love which replaces hate and comfort replaces lone-liness or that abandoned feeling that once robbed someone of their safety and security in this world. So now the stage is ready for performance.

Later on in the relationship, she begins to visualize her thought process and then begins to act out her negative thinking pattern and therefore creates a negative relationship because something he does will trigger this memory. If she were conscious of this, she would therefore see that no one is perfect and that she attracted this person in her life so she could experience her negative thought process because it lives in her "I am". She has become her thought process. She has become this pain and unhappiness because she was not able to process the abandonment in a healthy way. Anger by her caretakers and her caretaker's previous experience with pain was transferred into her. Her care-takers and friends only followed a behavioral pattern that was taught to them by their caretakers and friends. Please do not misunderstand and go into the blame game as we all have passed on what we were taught. Blaming will not heal, it only continues to block the original emotion to heal and that is ANGER.

Again, to break this DNA pattern, we must become conscious of our thoughts that will eventually manifest and produce the ACTION perform-ance by being positive thoughts. One healing method is to love uncon-ditionally. This does break the controlling negative pattern that our Egos loved to consistently manifest. It takes work but it can be done. It really depends on how much you want to heal your life and create a pure con-scious manifestation. To be awake and aware can create a harmonious life!

Creating affirmations and the Law of Attraction

These are more than just positive thoughts. They form the basics with which to change your beliefs. So how do we create positive affirmations? Ask yourself what you want, what you want to do. It is not just as simple as creating positive affirmations, you need to add feeling. Feelings add the fuel to the engine.

Lets take a look at how we ad feeling to our affirmations. The affirmation - I am a positive person - has no feeling. But if we now change it to - I am a happy and positive person who is positive in all situations – do you see the difference?

We need more than just fuel. We also require a spark to light the fuel. The affirmation is only in our conscious. Therefore, we need to move from conscious to subconscious. How do we achieve this? One of the best ways is with Mediation. Be clear about what you ask for. Always ask or create what is good for your higher purpose. If something isn't working for you, then there is not enough energy in your thought process that permits this to happen or it's not for your higher purpose.

CHAPTER TEN

The Conscious Creation Process

This creation space is where you begin the stages right before the Law of Attraction. This is where you practice in dis-creating negative thought and creating positive thought. This is where you become aware of the conditionings in your life and how these conditions created exactly the negative patterns you keep seeing in your life. You manifested it! What you send out will mirror back to you directly from the Universe. Remember, you create your experience. This is the stage where you clearly make your intent in anything you want in life. We do not ask the Universe for things we really do not need. Your own vibration of energy is aware of this.

So you want to own your own business and the business costs X amount of dollars to get it going. You've been doing your intent to manifest, but the bank says you do not have the kind of money to open the business. What I speak of here is that if you want this business, you have to empower to consciously create it. Visualize it, become totally aware that you own this business you are creating. You are sending out to the Universe and the Universe will mirror this back to you by opening gateways for you to accomplish this intent. Ask and you shall receive good. Know that your creation has been intended and released. When you intend for something to come to you, you must let go. You must know that what you requested has already been granted. Know it is on its way to you. Again, if it doesn't happen, there is either an unconscious doubt that has not been dis-created or it's not for your higher good.

Your outer world will begin to change and you will take action toward obtaining your dreams. Is it sounding too simple? It's not. The hardest part will be for you to dis-create all the negative thinking patterns you have accumulated over the years that kept you away from being in the driver's seat and creating your dream world.

We build on manifestation by seeing the results of our positive creative thoughts! When we visualize that our thought processes have changed our direction in life from a pattern of mishaps and misery to a happy and blissful life, then we want to keep building on that creation.

"There is a natural sequence to the Conscious Creation Process. This sequence begins when you are willing to experience your inner spiritual potential through the awareness that you are the creator of your thoughts."

DEEPAK CHOPRA

We always create from the unseen to the seen and from the invisible to the visible. What is in front of you has no power over you. One of our human issues is we think we are our thoughts and this can be suffering if those thoughts are negative. We are the creators of our thoughts. When we create a thought, we let go. And so it is manifested through the mirror of the Universe and the Law of Vibration. Once we create beautiful thoughts then we become the thought through the energy of vibration.

For example: I was abandoned by my father. The thought still lives within me. I attract men who abandon me. Another example: I always thought I had to live my responsibilities, even if I am not happy. I learned this in Sunday school while listening to a sermon. I believed in it, so it became my thought. I also attracted in relationships that I was not happy in because my thoughts became a responsibility no matter what the consequence. My beliefs create my experiences, so when I create a belief, I am automatically attracting in that experience. This is Law of Attraction.

"Many people have missed a profound truth about success. Success depends more on who you are than on what you do!"

DEEPAK CHOPRA

We are victims of our identity and beliefs. We identify with the roles we play. You are not your human identity. You are a spiritual *BEING* having a human experience. When we identify with roles, we lose power.

If you modify your beliefs, you can have different experiences. A spiritual conscious creator has beliefs that they manifest. Examples are: All my needs are met. I am the source of my abundance. I am one with Light.

There are many different belief levels. Belief levels can go from believing in fear based thoughts, a need of security, beliefs that were created by human law. Even some believe in Scientific Facts and rely on science to prove their belief. On these belief levels, you are unaware that you have consciously created them. We create our reality.

Conscious Creation has many cycles. We teach this in our workshops and also in individual sessions. There is the Unconscious, Dis-Creation and Conscious Creation.

Unconscious = unconsciously creating life until you awaken that you have co-created positive and negative experiences as your beliefs create your reality.

Dis-Creation = taking an inventory of our core negative beliefs and consciously choosing to dis-create negative beliefs and sub-vocalizing. You want to stop unconscious programming and re-program conscious positive beliefs.

Conscious Creation = when you clean the slate of your mind, you can consciously create what you wish to experience. Your creation can malfunction because it's in your mind. The mind can only create a relationship based on what it already knows. Your mind associates with both the negative and positive relationships you have already experienced. Your mind contains a file folder on all that has happened.

You must learn what it is you are sub-vocalizing so you can dis-create the negative pattern from this unconscious voice. They say that most of your core beliefs were programmed before you were five years old. You must come to understand your fears and hear when your negative beliefs are sub-vocalizing. You experience triggers because your unconscious mind is sub-vocalizing. You must train yourself to FEEL and HEAR when you are unconsciously creating. This is how you can dis-create.

Below is the verbal wording to the distinctive meditation. I always suggest recording it in your own voice as this is the most effective healing. To listen back to your own voice will help you gain speed to a conscious awakening. You can also purchase it from the Holistic Learning Center: http://www.holisticlearningcenter.com/

The Purpose For The Three Phases Of The Spiritual Distinction Meditation Are:

Phase One: Relaxes you, while it also begins to train your Ego-Mind to obey your *Spirit* as you command your mind to override your normal way of breathing.

Phase Two: Quiets your mind talk by directing your attention to your senses so that you can rehab your feelings how to process your environment through your five senses and feelings.

Phase Three: Teachers you how to FEEL the difference between your composite parts; specifically the difference between your *Spirit* and body, body and vision, *Spirit* and Ego-mind.

SPIRITUAL DISTINCTION MEDITATION

The Spiritual Distinction Meditation needs to be the first "disciplina" that you master, because it will synergistically affect all of your other Self-mastery skills.

PHASE ONE: Breathe & Relax...

Sit comfortably and close your eyes. Take a moment to consciously declare your intention to "feel" the difference between your Spirit, body, vision, and mind. Then relax and take three long, slow, deep breaths, inhaling through your nose to the count of seven, holding your breath to the count of seven. As you're doing this pinpoint your attention on commanding your mind to focus on the difference between how your breath feels when you inhale and how it feels when you exhale.

PHASE TWO: Feel your Body Senses...

Next, listen to the faintest sound that you can hear. Then take a few more seconds and listen for an even fainter sound. Next, inhale through your nose and notice what you *SMELL* (food, grass, candle, perfume). Next, swish your tongue around inside your mouth and between your gums, and notice what you can *TASTE* (salty, sour, sweet, or bitter). Next, *FEEL* the skin on the back of your hand between your knuckles and your wrist as lightly as you can. Notice how sensitive your sense of touch actually is. Your skin protects your body n the same way that your Ego-Mind protects your psyche, but with one exception; your Ego-Mind is a thousand times more sensitive than your skin.

PHASE THREE:

Feel the difference between...How your *Body Feels* and how your *Spirit Feels.*

Next, focus your attention on your *BODY* by moving it...lift your legs, pinch your skin, make a fist and move your head around. Feel how thick, heavy, and solid your body feels. Next, feel your *SPIRIT* by rapidly breathing in and out very assertively (rebirthing style) at least three to five times until you create a minor altered state of consciousness by unbalancing your oxygen/carbon dioxide gases (if you do this correctly, if should feel mildly uncomfortable). As you exhale your last breath, try not to breathe for at least ten-seconds. Now just feel what you are feeling, this is your *Spirit.* Just feel how the light vibration of *Spirit* feels. Now *FEEL* the difference between how your *SPIRIT* feels and how your *Body* feels by making a fist (which will bring your attention back to your body) so that you can compare how different they feel.

(Pause for ten seconds to feel the difference)

Feel the difference between… How Your Body Feels and how your Vision Feels.

Next, pick a **VISION** that is easy for you to visualize like a car, house, person, or beach. Create it with as much detail as possible. Make the vision so real that you can pick up something and feel that it has weight. Now smell it and put it against your skin and feel its temperature. Notice that in your **VISION** you perceive height, depth, width, sound, weight, tempera-ture, and even odor. Now feel your **BODY** again, actually feel it (make a fist). Feel how similar your body and vision feel. Lastly, feel the subtle dif-ference between the weight of the molecules of your body and the weight of the molecule in your vision (which is much lighter).

(Pause for ten seconds to feel the difference)

Feel the difference between… How Your Ego-Mind Feels and how your Spirit Feels

Next, notice that your *MIND* is always sub-vocalizing (talking inside your head). Notice what your *MIND* is saying right now (pause). Be sure that you catch what your mind is saying. Do not accept general answers like: "my mind is quiet." This is usually an indication that you can't distinguish between your intuitive Self and your mind talk. Your mind never stops talking. It's always concerned with what you should be doing, what you didn't do, what you could so, and what someone else did. Talk, talk, and talk! Your mind is addicted to excitement and you can usually feel it in your stomach area, like when you go down the first hill of a roller coaster and you feel that "Wooooooooh" feeling. Now just feel how you feel when your Ego-Mind is doing its "think-think fear act.") Feel your ego's uptight, stressful energy (pause to feel it).

Next, repeat the same procedures that you did to feel your *SPIRIT* by rapidly breathing in and out, very assertively, at least three to five times until you create a minor altered state of consciousness. When you exhale your last breath, do nothing but feel your *Spirit*. Feel the quiet, light vibration of *Spirit*. Next, focus your attention on feeling the difference between how your *Spirit* feels and how Your Ego-Minds feels. Notice that your Ego-Mind is the talker, and your *SPIRIT* is the listener (pause for ten seconds to feel the difference). Spend a few minutes enjoying this state of bliss by focusing your "feelings" on the different sensations of inhaling and exhaling. Then when you feel complete, you can open your eyes.

Do this meditation daily if you can. It will assist you in finding truth within first and then in your outer world. Remember the memory chip in your mind and within your physical body. It plays out in your emotional body and is put into action. By being aware of this, you will be able to access a great deal of what has lied dormant within you and what you have been acting out throughout your life.

When you dis-create, do not judge. This is very important! If you do, you just went into Ego again and then you will attract more parasites on to the emotion that surfaced. In this book, I will be listing a variety of questions and I want you to journal everything. Writing is a good way to release and it also helps you to see the changes you need to make consciously. Writing also helps you to go beyond the clutter of your mind and manifest beautiful things for yourself. You can really get creative when writing as also using art to bring out the negativity in you and re-create.

CHAPTER ELEVEN

Visualization

Visualization is part of the conscious creation process. Get visual. Really see what you want to create and happen. You are your own Director, Producer and Script Writer. Write the script, see it on the movie screen and send it out to be produced! If you have a hard time visualizing, as really you are not, you just think that you can't visualize, just KNOW it has been created. FEEL IT! BREATHE IT! Visualizing is a part of awareness. When we are aware with all our inner senses, we can then feel are presence in our creation. We become the BEING or the, I am.

Here is an exercise for awareness and visualization that includes the 5 senses.

Imagine that you are holding a Rose in your hand. Let your imagination go. Really visualize (sight) the Rose. When you are done observing the Rose, feel the texture of it in your hands. Be aware (touch) of how your hands feel holding this Rose. Now study the Rose further in your hands. You are in present moment. Let it guide you.

After some moments, allow yourself to smell the Rose. Feel what it feels like smelling the Rose. Let your imagination roam with the smell of the

Rose. What senses are you aware of when smelling the Rose? Next, taste the Rose. What does tasting the Rose feel like in your mouth? What senses are you aware of when tasting the Rose? Now listen (sound) to the Rose. What messages does she give you? What does she speak to you? Now go inside the Rose and feel how it is to be that Rose. Feel all the beauty as a Rose. Go through the 5 senses as if you are the Rose.

After some time, come out of the Rose and feel the Rose as the center of your surroundings. How does the Rose uplift the vibration in the room? What messages are you getting? Listen. Always breathe freely. Be conscious of your breath. Pay attention to your feelings. Pay attention to your emotions. Remember to breathe rapidly if an emotion arises and you begin to feel anxiety. Anxiety is caused by fear or an emotion that has been overwhelming.

When we are angry, we manifest anger. When we are happy, we manifest happiness. Always feel what comes to you. Do not deny it. Denial is Ego trying to avoid or protect FEAR. The importance of consciously creating your dreams, manifesting them is to really feel what you want to create. Honestly, we cannot be consciously creative for our higher good unless we can feel what we want to create. You can put a lot of light and power behind an emotion.

I am posting some questions here that are important. Answer these questions and be as honest as you can. Feel deeply and write all the negative answers first. Do not go back and read it. Returning to the thoughts you just released is like re-living them again. Then after you are done, don't wait, start writing what you want to change, keeping in mind that this is what you are consciously creating NOW. Don't expect that what you write in both categories will be enough. This is hard work and the foundation of changing your thoughts is what you intend to create and send out to manifest. You will be creating one-step at a time into your thoughts and you will begin to manifest. When you write, write meaningfully.

We didn't absorb millions of negative thoughts against a thousand positive thoughts in a day! It took some years to absorb those negative thoughts. We must work together in consciously creating beautiful thoughts. What you will start with is always a blessing. The more you go and repeat this exercise, the more you will get even deeper. Use the meditation provided here to your benefit, even if it hurts. If you are feeling pain and you were unable to jot down the visions of *CHANGE*, then return again later or the next day. Don't be shy in asking. Don't be shy in creating. Let your imagination flourish. But be heart centered. Make it a part of your everyday calendar to master your Spirit over your Ego. You have to really give yourself a push here. We get set in our ways, and habits are hard to break.

The first body feeling you may experience is rejection. Your body has memories because within your solar plexus, you have another mind. This is your body's physical mind. What is absorbed in your subconscious is also absorbed into your body's physical mind. Have you ever experienced a trauma or heartbreak and all you could feel was it sitting in your stomach? You begin to experience anxiety, nausea, heartburn, butterflies or even pain. This is your solar plexus and behind the stomach, pancreas and liver is your body's physical mind. Physical memories are stored here also. Then they are passed along and absorbed through our muscles, tissues and cells. When healing our mind in our heads, we also synchronize to heal the mind in the physical body. When we are touching core deep, our body sends out triggers. Your mind may be peaceful, but your body may be roaring like a Lion. Why is this? Because your body is sending out signals to your mind in your head that it has remembered an occasion or situation that you had once experienced and the triggers and sensations are like warning signs. When conscious of this, you can really control the triggers by saying you are *here* and *now*. It's also good to ask yourself, why am I feeling this sensation in this location? For example you feel pain or a sense of weakness in your right arm while releasing Ego and becoming Spirit. You may ask your arm, why are you feeling this way? What memories do I surface when I feel the pain and weakness in my right arm?

FEAR (False Evidence Appearing Real) will try to stop you but remember *FEAR* is not real. By being in present moment, you can master *FEAR* as in presence, Spirit does not want the *Ego* to master. Its natural birthright is to be free of conditions, pain and judgment. In psychology, they call the physical feelings as triggers. Someone who has been in a car accident, for example watches a movie that has scenes of trauma and they begin to feel a sensation that may take them back in memory to that moment they had the accident. The body begins to feel pain or becomes extremely restless. These are called triggers, triggering a memory. Don't try to be a martyr as this will not give you the opportunity to heal and process your healing. It's very important to communicate with all parts of your mental, emotional and physical bodies.

Another example would be all the chitter-chatter that goes on in one's head during the onstage of meditation. When the chitter-chatter begins mentally, put up a mental movie screen and then sit back and watch it without judging it on the screen. Or let the chitter-chatter go on but do not listen or judge it. Let it speak or let it play through. Don't fear in what you may feel, see or hear. Don't fight it. Let it just flow because I guarantee it will weaken. The Ego cannot survive in a non-judgmental environment. Don't worry about feeling hurt or pain. I know that it is not easy to feel this emotion. It can be very uncomfortable for many. But if you can accept that what happened, happened, you will find an inner sense of enlightenment. It's when we can't accept what happened to us that the internal arguments, fighting and repetitive behavioral patterns continue to exist.

Answer these questions honestly. After answering these questions, immediately go to what you would like to attract in. Put a lot of power in it! Really go deep and pull out those negative thoughts, pain, sorrow, confusion and so on. Then when writing out all you desire, know that what you just created is done! Become those positive thoughts. All that I am telling you here is so divine magical. Let go of the judgments of yourself and others. Be free when speaking to the Universe. Send out amazing and brilliant thoughts. Get creative for your higher *BEING*. Remember, that you create your experience. Become your thought instantly!

Below are questions that I feel are important to help you open your mind so that you can get deep.

1. Are you comfortable in your life? In your mind? In your body? Are you happy?
2. What are your relationship patterns? What do they reflect in you? Are you happy?
3. How do you perceive yourself? How do others perceive you? How do people react to you?
4. Are you aware of any patterns of self-destruction?
5. Do you feel victimized by anyone or thing?
6. What are your fears? Why?

Answer each question, one at a time. Take as long as you need without fooling yourself. Don't rush through this thinking that you need to finish this book in order to manifest, because you do not!

After you have written and released your unconscious, go immediately to writing the change in consciousness. Write all the wonderful things you want in your life. Write it in present moment. Use the first party, "I" or "I AM" = BEING. BE-IN-G-D=Divine.

Here is an example of something I wrote. It's on relationship patterns. I wrote down all the things I felt I suffered from, how others treated me, etc. Then after I felt I was finished (it feels good to do this too!), I went immediately to writing all the things I wanted to create as if I already had them in my life. Do not go back and read what you wrote. You already released as you wrote it, dis-creating all those unconscious negative thoughts, pain, sorrow, anger, blame and so on. By going back and reading what you wrote is equal to revisiting the past and strengthening it as if it just happened yesterday. Believe in the power of thought.

I feel it's important to feel what you wrote. Feelings give us answers in Spirit as thinking does in Ego. If you can remain in feeling your responses, rather than thinking, you will get beyond your ego-confined ways. Understand that you give power to your thoughts as well as your words. You saw the patterns once you wrote them down. By going directly into re-creating, you are manifesting. You leave no space between dis-creating and re-creating. Never give the mind time to rationalize when you want to manifest because if you do, your Ego will come up and put it on hold and you are back to square one. You switch on the subconscious to release, then switch off for a few breaths and switch on the conscious. You are bringing forth conscious and unconscious thoughts, then resting just a second and then switching back on into conscious creating.

You will fall and bruise your knees but you will get up and walk again. Do not let self pity or denial keep you from being your own Creator. The Creator lives within you. Deal with your fears heart on, not head on. Feel your spirit. Stay conscious. The past has already been lived and gone. Memories are all you have and they have been repeated thousands of times if not more and re-lived every time you remember them. And through re-living them, they have become more powerful. You attract in what you are thinking and then it becomes you and your outer world. You manifest your thoughts. Be in present when you create and release. Become your newly created thoughts.

Here are a few steps to remind you. Keep them handy

1. Get Present.
2. Take a step back (dis-create).
3. Notice how you are feeling.
4. Observe your thoughts without judgment.
5. Question their validity.
6. Let go of what could, should, and would have been.
7. Release the what-ifs.
8. Love yourself. (not your identity self or ego self)
9. There is only NOW.
10. Feel the presence of your heart.
11. Make only decisions that feel good.

CHAPTER TWELVE

Creation

Here is what Omraam Mikhael Anahov has to say: "*Thought can pass through walls and physical objects without a trace; in order to get it to take effect on the material level, you have to build bridges, that is to say, a series of intermediaries. Send it through these intermediaries and you will see that it is capable of shaking the universe to its foundations. This is the meaning of that famous saying of Archimedes: 'Give me a lever and I will move the earth!' The lever is an intermediary and an intermediary is always necessary. Thought is powerful and effective on condition that the intermediaries are there to allow it to descend all the way to the level of matter.*"

So thought works like this. It begins in the mental plane and then travels to the Astral Plane. Once it gets to Astral, it's ready to travel to the Etheric, and then to Matter. So you have to get your thoughts down from the mental plane to the Astral before you can manifest. Here is the spelled out formula. Thought (Emotion-Intent-Mind) = Law of Vibration (sending it out-force of energy-manipulating the energy to send it out quick and with gratitude) = Word (you choose to use words as words can be very powerful. Your words must be impeccable). = Deed (Action)! Once you release your Vibration power (energy) then let go. Know it is in the works and you must become the action of the seed you just planted through space and time.

A great many people have ideas, but they live in such a way that there is never any connection between their ideas and their actions. There must be an intermediary, a bridge, and that intermediary is feeling, emotion. When it enters the dimension of the emotions, an idea then takes on energy and becomes capable of influencing matter.

The spirit acts on thought, thought, in turn, acts on the feelings, and the feelings surge into the physical body, causing it to move, to make a gesture, to speak. This is where you have the power. The physical body, therefore, is moved by feeling, feeling is aroused by thought and thought is born through the influence of the spirit.

Omraam Mikhael Anahov uses the arm as an example: An arm is the intermediary between a thought and an object. When I pick up a lump of sugar, which is actually performing the action? My thought is performing the action. Yes, through the arm that serves as its intermediary, it is my thought that is acting. And suppose my thought remains inactive; what then? I still have an arm, but if there is no thought and no desire to stimulate it to take a lump of sugar, it will not do so. It is in this sense that one can speak of the power of thought.

One thing that prevents human beings from understanding the effects of their thoughts and feelings is the fact that these effects are not immediately apparent. But you should not need immediate effects in order to be convinced. People say, 'We can't see any of that; it is impossible to believe it!' Initiates, on the other hand, have taken the time and trouble to observe, examine and verify what happens in nature, and they know that everything ends by coagulating, condensing.

Here is an example of how I get things down on paper and what I do from that point on. I take a blank piece of paper or a journal. I never limit myself on what I am going to write. I want to have as much room as I possibly can because one thought will lead to another. Thoughts are like magnets. I begin to write all the things that bother me from love to my weight. I write on anything, all things that seem to bother me or have stopped me in some way. I write them very quickly. Get emotional and really draw in the hard core pains you have felt through life. I do not give myself time to think about what I write. Write as fast as you can. Do not stop and think about what to write or read what you wrote.

After I am finished, I breathe deep once or twice, get present and go right into what I want to create (Switch on dis-creation, Switch off, Switch on creation). It might seem simple to you but it does have a catch. If it were that simple to create anything we wanted, we would all be doing it and there would be no complaints. You will touch upon some very deep and emotional core issues that you have carried along your journey. Start by forgiving yourself. Let go of the guilt. This is about you, even though you may be writing about your mother, father, husband or children. One of the biggest purposes here is to let go of past conditions that you have accepted along the way that are stopping you on your road to a successful life. I keep writing at a fast pace using occasionally the "I AM" or "I HAVE." I never use "I WANT" or "I WISH" because then you are telling the Universe not to mirror back anything concrete. You are not in present moment with wanting and wishing. I am not saying to want or wish is bad, just it is not living NOW.

I visualize all I am creating. I know and am firm that this exists in my world. So I am linking the two together. You can't be the observer here. You must be the visionary. Visionaries succeed, observers may succeed but when things get difficult, they revert back to suffering and get rutted in thought. There are occasional obstacles on our path, understand that they are learning lessons and challenges. Meet them thought on and change them to work with you, not against you. You might find that after doing this exercise, there might be some adversary to your thought process. The reason is you had created before you did this exercise. Might be too late to change it but one thing for sure, you will certainly be aware of what manifests before your new creation and you will just have to go and dis-create and re-create.

Once you have completed the creation process, let go. Know it is done and you have it. If you do not, some doubt from past experience will block it. Letting go is a great part of manifesting. Don't sit around and wait for it. Know it will be yours. In the Universe, there is no time. On earth is where our time zone exists. We are conditioned to believe in time. If time is an essence for you, then set a time with your manifestation. I prefer not to. I just know it's done and on its way. Always create your intentions in the *NOW*. If you have set a time for your manifestation, be clear as to what you want and be clear when you want it. Everything you create is important. Be conscious of what you are creating so that you do not create something you do not want. Make sure that you have cleared the slate (mind) and there are no attachments, such as visualizing a new place to live, but then the chitter-chatter (mental chattering) begins and says you can't afford a mortgage. See what I mean? Be very sure of all you put out there and that it is on its way to you *NOW* with no *DOUBT*.   Live it, breathe it, and accept it.

Now that the motion is set in creation, this is the Law of Attraction. There is no special entity or space for Law of Attraction. Law of Attraction is Vibration. Vibration of energy happens all the time. It happens every second with the thoughts we create. That is why it is so important to be conscious of what you are creating. Just create but be aware of what is still negative in your mind. The more you are conscious of what comes to you and what your thought process attracts and creates, the more you will see your dreams come true.

If something doesn't feel good, ask your inner self, what is it that makes me feel this way? You will get your answer. When you feel a body symptom, ask that part of your body to remember what thought or action caused you to feel this way? You will get to the memory. Always remember to breathe through difficult feelings, even rapid breathing such as the *Holotropic* breath work or *rebirthing* breath work. When you come across something that you feel burdened by mentally or physically, then say, I let go of....It no longer serves my higher purpose as a Divine Being. Remember to stay present in the *HERE AND NOW*.

I have given you one good example of how to dis-create negative belief patterns and re-create healthy ones to assist you in manifesting all that you want. If you practice this method, you will get very good at creating. You will also become more aware of your thoughts. We can be spontaneous. Why rush into anything? It's very important that you process. We can easily self-destruct, as we have been taught to self-destruct. When we come across emotions we have already experienced, and they are negative emotions, we can self-destruct if we do not process what has happened... happened. We get into that "pity" mood. Then we set the pattern of feeling sorry for ourselves. I'm not saying that what you feel, even if feeling low isn't how you really feel. It's just that we have been conditioned to feel pain first rather than bliss. We have been conditioned to feel life is complicated rather than be grateful for all we feel, have and are. Trauma is probably one of the most difficult emotions to let go of. It not only lives in memory, but it also lives in the physical body. As mentioned before, the body also has a physical memory as well as a mind. You can let go. We can let go of anything. You just have to accept what has happened…happened.

Understand this: Think a thought. Manifestation will happen. Think a thought; feel an emotion, manifestation happens! Think a thought with emotion…MANIFESTATION HAPPENS FAST!!! (This is the Law of Vibration… the Law of Attraction).

CHAPTER THIRTEEN

Understanding the Power of Positive Feelings

You have gone through awareness, visualization and dis-creating and re-creating energy and thought. You feel a power within you and strength to feel it through. You feel an energy inside that talks its own language and you feel this energy that gives you strength and yet you feel you were born to do something but yet you can't put your thought on just what it is you were born to do. You feel yourself walk into any situation, confident and at peace. You feel successful. When we greet someone, we say, "Hello" and, "How are you?" or "How are you feeling today?" Have you noticed that we never ask, "How are we thinking today?" or, "What have you been thinking?"

We live how we feel, in my opinion. If the weather outside is gloomy, many of us feel gloomy. If it's cloudy, they feel their life is cloudy. If the sun shines, they are thanking God that the sun is shining as they can't take another depressed day. How true is this? I hear it all the time. I, at one time, was like this, too. This conditional feeling has also been passed to us through our DNA. Our ancestors were definitely affected by the environment as they lived more in the world and of it than the opposite. Understand that living in the world and of it, means you become all the worlds issues. Even your own outer world becomes your current issues. As mentioned before, you become your outsourced problems. Whatever you are feeling, your life reflects that feeling. If I feel miserable, my life reflects that misery. If I feel successful, my life becomes successful. Every moment, we feel something. Am I right?

Indeed. These feelings shape our destiny every moment. There's nothing wrong with feeling.

Feeling focuses on thinking. When we think, a feeling develops. If I feel stressed, then I become stressed. If I think about all those bills I need to pay this month, my body gets tense because I am thinking that I have to spend money, I may not have. Do you see the pattern? I am already thinking I do not have enough money to pay the pile of bills sitting on the other end of my desk. However, you think, so be your outcome. You will react accordingly, guaranteed.

Our thoughts manifest. If you do not believe me, here is a good example of a thought that manifested and not only manifested it transferred to each person in that room. A man had a bad day at work. The more he thought about how bad his day was going, the worse the day got. A few co-workers came by his desk and tried to cheer him up, but he would not release the negative thinking and so the light that others shared with him could not transfer over. Thoughts do transfer. In telepathy, we know we can send thoughts and thoughts are received. When the work day ended, the man went home to his family. When he walked in the door, in a matter of seconds, the room filled with sadness. Everyone felt his energy. Because as the day progressed, the more negative the man became. He continued to moan and complain around the house and soon arguments happened and everyone was feeling unhappy. This is thought transfer. Again a thought becomes a feeling. This demonstrates Law of Attraction in motion.

Thinking positive has limitations. If I asked you what your next thought was, you would have to think about it before you could answer me. Most people reflect on their past. What they've already experienced. Too much thinking leads you right into your past. The past is what you have lived and it's in memory. And the past has already been lived, so *NOW* what? *NOW* equals living this very moment. Nothing else matters. Not the past or the future. The past is your illusion and so is the future. If you focus on the past or future, you have missed the moment. It's the moment that creates your future. The very next moment after *NOW*, is the future. The Monks and Yogis practice this ritual. If you jump to that very next moment, you have lost center field. You have only a right and a left. The mind gets confused. Your Spirit will know which direction to choose. It feels the wisdom that is centered. It's the Ego that wants to set you sailing into the past or concerns of the future which hasn't even arrived. I am not saying it's bad to daydream and think of a successful future. But you are mirroring the Universe the future without a base hit in center field. Means you are not *BEING* your dreams *NOW*. So not *BEING* in *NOW* means nothing (no-thing) creates.

There are many who re-live the past every day. By returning and re-living your past it is like it just happened and get's stronger with each visit. But this is an illusion because the past has already been lived. It's not happening any longer. You are just re-living memories in your head and your Ego is keeping it alive. And I can guarantee that the memories have received more attachments each time they are remembered and re-lived, because the past no longer exists and the Judge and the Victim in your head has assumed many roles attached to this memory. The memory of the past just got bigger. And soon it feels as though it takes up three-quarters of your life.

Change how you feel in the moment. Nothing else is important. As adults, we have learned to accept failure. As a child we know no failure. So what happened between us as a child and adulthood? We accepted the word, we accepted the programming and from there we accepted a limited life. If you want to achieve a breakthrough in any area of your life, feel yourself first, then let go. Let your feelings come out so that you do not reprogram the same negative thoughts that continuously stop your life. Think too much? You bet you do! And what do you usually think about? Your feelings. I am also sure you have heard the phrase, "History repeats itself"? Literally, how many say this phrase? It's true, history does repeat itself and that's because the same old DNA patterns keep repeating until you change it.

So how do we let go of a thought? How do we let go of a feeling that reflects a thought? You can learn to let these feelings go after you discover where they come from in the first place. A person who has trust issues feels insecure and generally not safe in the world. Why? Because they do not trust because they are thinking of what they do not trust and feeling memories attached to not trusting. How can you not trust an experience you haven't lived yet? The very first reaction will be your Ego and it will remind you that that's all you know. Your subconscious memory will tell you that you have lived this experience before and it has caused you either pain or harm in some way. As long as you think of the past, the longer you will stay out of the moment and into *FEAR*. Fear is not real (False Evidence Appearing Real). How many times have you lived this *FEAR* of non-trust and actually created it into your partner in a relationship until it becomes very real?

The power lies within you. Always, this is your birthright. It's up to you to change the negative feelings into positive feelings. Once you do this, you will also reprogram your mind to accept "good feelings".

Understand that you can also intend something for the future, but why would you want to do that? By the time you get to that time line, anything can change. You do not even know when you will reach that intent as the future is an illusion. You can't live the future if you haven't lived the moment.

CHAPTER FOURTEEN

The Power of Being YOU! I Can Be What I Will Be, The Divine Power, "I am".

From this base "I am" becomes *Divine Power.* Any person can be *Power.* We are all great. Your objects and purpose must be constructive and follow the Laws of The Universe. "I Can Be What I will Be, Divine Power". Any work of power that is not in coherence with Divine Law and Power will not flourish. There is a Principle of Divine Power in every person. To be Divine power within has tremendous force and effect in your life. This is the seat of the Omniscience and Infinite flow. A Genius is in understanding that the Divine power within holds the key to All Possibilities. We are all geniuses when we live within and know that the power cannot be sought outside of ourselves. The "I am" presence is exact, and the "I am" rules within us as we are all born with it and is connected to our birthright. It cannot be overruled.

One must convert all their human will power over to the Divine Power within. Free will can choose but must be in balance with the Divine Power within. Having Divine Power becomes complete awareness within and knows only within, and constructs a healthy and vital power that creates his outer world by the "I". "I" is the seat of the soul and knows how to work the power of vibration and it's living in the cause and effect. It's the soul's birthright. Self denial is not success as many are led to believe. The Infinite begins with "I" and is not bankrupt from within. The outer world is not bankrupt when living Omnipresence within. The "I" within has the key to master anything within and so reflects the outer world.

Divine Power within allows the Universe to express, through us and actively be of service to humanity. By strengthening your Divine seat, one cannot be controlled, but only develop his own mental faculties. One who understands and completes Divine Power within understands each Law and abides by them, creating immaculate growth and success.

Divine power creates larger than one's deeds. Being in Divine seat is Dharma and Universe balanced within. Divine Power has an inherent power by which it may grow within us whatsoever direction the "I" pleases, and there does not appear to be any limit to the possibilities of Universal growth. The possibility is the Original Substance from which man is made. Genius is Omniscience flowing into man. Genius is the union of man and Divine in the acts of the soul. It is all and all possibilities. The soul is in connection with a reserve power that is without limit. It is ALL and abiding. It must not be tampered with as it knows all within and is sure of its direction. We do not know where the boundary of the mental powers of higher Divinity is; we do not even know that there is a boundary.

The Universe cannot express itself through you if you are busy with anxieties of the world. If you live in the world and are of it you will not find the Divine Power within you. Living in the world and not being of it will assist your activation in Divine Power. We become Divine conscious power and create a substantial Divine world only living within.

Divine Power is magical and is the Creator of all things. All this lives within us and it's up to us to activate the "I" within us to meet the Omnipresence of the Divine Seat. The Results of living in Divine Power.

- Less stress or ZERO stress.
- More financial abundance as "I" manifests all that is of service.
- Deeper, more loving relationships. Relationships become unconditional.
- Better health, wellness and vitality. All healing is active.
- Career success. One knows no boundaries in success. We are breathing and living the results of Divine Power within.
- Bliss, Peace, happiness and more.

Happiness and success are equally available to everyone when you learn how to release the blocks, the thoughts and feelings, and limitations you hold. Divine Power is the key to Self Mastery because *Self* becomes the "I" only.

CHAPTER FIFTEEN

Law of Attraction

Remember thought is motion and is carried by the Law of Vibration. It is given vitality and emotions through LOVE. What is the secret power? The secret power is service. Why so? We get what we give.

Your thoughts must be pure. The Law of Attraction is "Like attracts like". The Law of Attraction is one thought in a matter of seconds. Many look for an entire workbook on Law of Attraction but it is the Law of Vibration moving your thoughts through emotion and the Law of LOVE that manifests. Vibration is energy and it moves all the time.

Law of Attraction can be completed in 16 seconds or less. This is the Law of Attraction. Once you have completed the thought process, it has been sent out and completed. There is a chance to cancel your thought once it has been sent out. But you must be aware of it immediately.

Our world is being destroyed by negative conscious transmission. If the thought is not pure then it is full of parasites. All previous thoughts are in the process of manifestation but can be dis-created and re-created at any-time. You must show your sincerity in the conscious process to be able to cancel or clear out previous manifestations that were not for your higher good. If this has happened, then the dis-creation process will assist you on how to dis-create negative thought patterns and re-create positive, healthy thoughts and actions.

All that I have explained in this book have everything to do with creating a blissful world within you and having your inner essence create your outer world.   It is important to be conscious of all you think, speak and act. Have you heard of the phrase, actions speak louder than words? It does. It is the "cause and effect". Action stimulates the thought process that was sent out by believing and knowing it has been completed and living in "I AM' within. Action is the physical motion of your manifestation. If you just sit there waiting for things to happen, you will miss life. Putting the wheels of thought and action in motion complete the Law of Attraction.

Follow the steps I have given and you will create a life of bliss. The Universe will mirror all beautiful things through you. All your dreams of living in present moment and manifesting all you want…will happen.

CONCLUSION

The Pathway to Bliss

Anyone who may be interested in hosting a workshop in Conscious Creation, Law of Attraction and Manifestation, please contact us at www. thepathwaytobliss.com. All individual sessions/classes can also be provided in a workshop. We service small, medium, large and corporate businesses. We also work with individuals in Self Mastery, Relationship Mastery, Money Mastery, Spiritual Sales, Telepathy/Soul Connection, Healing and more. Please note, "About the Author" on the following page for more information. If interested in any of our services, please contact us at www. thepathwaytobliss.com

About The Author

Spirit Walker *is an accredited Spiritual Mentor, with an extensive background in Spiritual Counseling, Life Coaching in Self Mastery, Relationship Mastery, and Conscious Creation and the Law of Attraction. Her expertise is in the Spiritual-Higher Self, Mastery of Self, Relationships, Manifestation, Telepathy and The Spiritual Business Entrepreneur (How to consciously create your desires (soul core) and manifest the outcome (all that you need). She's intuitive and gives an accurate reading at soul-level and is quick to find a solution, drawing deep from the inner core of the BEING with the power to dis-create the negative behavioral patterns and re-create with the power of INTENT. She is owner and director of 3 successful companies and shares her knowledge and wisdom with whomever hires her expertise, confidentially.*

Spirit Walker *comes from a background in business that carries weight in the Corporate and Individual, Small/Medium-Business Industry. She has obtained many Awards and Trophies from her knowledge and application in Sales, Creative Application (Conscious Creation/Law of Attraction) and knowledge of Team-Soul Core communication (Telepathy). She also delivers key-emphasis on the 7 Spiritual Laws of the Universe in our lives and applied daily to all that we do. Her "global" experience and teachings are for all walks of life.*

Spirit Walker *has many years of experience delivering training, practical application, and coaching to many in a wide variety of professions, ie...Individual, Groups, Organizations, Small Businesses and Corporate Entrepreneurs. She is currently working on several books, geared to the audience in search of discovering their birthright.*

Her core-team shares the experience, knowledge and wisdom she has created and applied for the past 35 years. Just recently, her Supreme Guidance has given her a blessed-spiritual name..Spirit Walker.

Printed in Great Britain
by Amazon.co.uk, Ltd.,
Marston Gate.